Shakti

Barbara Pidgeon grew up in Scotland but has spent much of her adult life in several countries around the world. Throughout her international career, she always endeavoured to understand the diversity of the people she felt privileged to work and live amongst and would seek firsthand experience in local cultural and spiritual practices whenever possible. Her many enriching encounters over the years led her to a rural spot in Jharkhand, India, where she met her guru, Swami Satyasangananda, whose story she had the great honour to write about in this book.

Currently, she lives in London researching how we are impacted by the way that we breathe, a fascinating topic that we know so very little of, she argues, and one that she plans as the subject of her next book.

Shakti Manifest

A Silent Revolution

To Poppy
Truth is in you
Love is in you
You are in you

Barbara Pidgeon

Search for your own freedom

with love and grace

Barbara x

London 11 June 2015

Westland Ltd

westland ltd

61 Silverline Building, 2nd floor, Alapakkam Main Road, Maduravoyal, Chennai 600095

No. 38/10 (New No.5), Raghava Nagar, New Timber Yard Layout, Bangalore 560026

93, 1st Floor, Sham Lal Road, Daryaganj, New Delhi 110002

First published in India by westland ltd 2014

Copyright © Rikhiapeeth 2014

The proceeds accruing from sale of this book will be directly
made to the ashram to continue their work in the development
and upliftment of the young *kanyas* of Rikhia.

ISBN: 978-93-84030-29-2

Typeset by Ram Das Lal

Printed at Replika Press Pvt. Ltd.

This is dedicated to all women of the world
and, in particular, to:

My Guru
Paramhansa Swami Satyasangananda Saraswati

My Mother
Sadie

My Daugthers
Nicole
Yvonne
Ilaria
Tasneem
Raneem
Aisha
Sundous

Contents

Foreword

A Few Words by Swami Satyasangananda Saraswati,
Peethadhiswari, Rikhiapeeth, Jharkhand

While it is essentially true that women have enormous potential and have even been given the status of *Devi* in our land, Bharatvarsha, still the actual manifestation of this in the world will only take place when women themselves realise this. At present they don't. Women have tremendous power and compassion too. Women have inherent wisdom and innate beauty. Women are soft and gentle, loving and kind. They are full of grace, dignity and poise. They are tolerant, honest and obedient. Women are ambassadors, carrying goodwill, charm, expertise and diplomacy wherever they go. Women rise to the need of situations in a magnificent way however difficult they maybe. They have hidden reserves which come to the surface when they are touched, moved or inspired.

This book is inspired by womanhood. Written with the idea of celebrating the notion of women empowerment, it looks at the very unique way of uplifting women that Rikhiapeeth offers. By elevating the little girl child to the status of *kanya* here at Rikhiapeeth, revered Gurudev Pujya Paramhansa Satyananda, sowed the divine seed of liberation for women.

The Vedas declare that devas, the divine illumined beings, do not visit the place where women are not respected, adored and worshipped. This means that if our land becomes bereft of the idea of women as *kanya* or *devi* then, in course of time, this land will perish, decay and die. Thus, the idea of women empowerment is not just for women alone but for the future of our land, our nation, our values, our traditions and our very own identity.

This book is an effort to bring forth this idea by showing the example of Rikhiapeeth where this tradition of awakening for women is strongly establishing its roots. It is unique as the author has succeeded in interweaving many aspects of Swami Satyananda's vision, not just for women, but for society at large.

Rikhiapeeth is Swami Satyananda's gift to society. His social vision. His *sankalpa* and its beautiful enactment. I am happy that Barbara Pidgeon was inspired to present his vision to all and congratulate her for her perceptive talent of drawing out the essence of what Rikhiapeeth stands for, a lesson in LOVE.

May Guru's grace shine brightly in her life.

———

A Few Words by Swami Niranjanananda Saraswati, Paramacharya, Sannyaspeeth

Hari Om

The narratives in *Shakti Manifest* make the reader a witness to the unfolding of the vision of Sri Swami Satyananda Saraswati in the remote, unknown and unheard of village of Rikhia. Through his vision, Rikhiapeeth has become a focal point for the cultivation of spiritual awareness and the highest human qualities and skills, imbibed through living and practising the cardinal principals of Sri Swami Sivananda Saraswati – to serve, love and give.

Sanctified by the presence of Sri Swami Satyananda Saraswati who performed rigorous Vedic and Tantric *tapasya* and austerities there, Rikhiapeeth is a hallowed and sacred place, the energy of which is palpable and inspires all to experience the oneness of spirit. It has become a centre of human awakening where people connect with the selfless aspect of themselves and strive to bring joy and happiness in the lives of others in the nearby rural and tribal communities.

The vision of Sri Swami Satyananda which one sees manifest in Rikhiapeeth is the spiritual empowerment of the feminine gender – elevating women to the status of *Devi*, engendering within them an awareness of the positive contribution they can make as individuals to their families and society. This journey to realise and express the positive qualities of life begins in infancy, with the village children who come to the ashram, as part of Sri Swami Satyananda's *sankalpa* and become the *kanyas* and *batuks* of Rikhiapeeth.

The central figure of this luminous inspiration is Swami Satyasangananda. She herself represents the flowering of the highest spiritual teachings of to serve, love and give, a mandate given to her by her Guru, Sri Swami Satyananda, when he installed her as *Peethadishwari* of Rikhiapeeth in 2007, the final year of his Rajasooya Yajna.

Swami Satsangi's spiritual journey has not been a bed of roses. The road she took is the most demanding path, the razor's edge, where the entire personal ego and ambition is eventually surrendered, and it is the guru's grace and teaching which then shapes the disciple's life. Like a patient sculptor with illumined vision, Sri Swami Satyananda simply chipped away all the excess and superfluous stone, to reveal the inherent beauty hidden within. The ultimate test of a disciple is to accept all the blows of the Guru's chisel as he sculpts. Once this process is completed, the disciple becomes a pure channel, a conductor for the energy, the *shakti* and the teaching, the *shiksha* of the guru to flow through.

Today, due to the grace of her Guru, Swami Satyasangananda stands tall in the exalted line of female spiritual luminaries of India, as a modern-day saint in her own right, alongside Gargi, Maitreyi and female *sannyasins* of yore. This is an example of *shakti manifest*, where the guru is the transmitter and the disciple is the receiver.

The same manifestation of *shakti* is the vision for Rikhiapeeth which we behold in the flowering of the *kanyas* and *batuks* and the emergence of womankind as compassionate, understanding and spiritually qualified, ready to achieve great heights. Rikhiapeeth gives one an opportunity to explore the spiritual potential in life and discover the soft human qualities which allow one to explore the spiritual realms, while remaining aware of the material dimension of life.

I am happy that Barbara Pidgeon has written this fitting tribute and narration of her experiences and time at Rikhiapeeth, and am confident that this narrative will inspire womankind to discover and express the beauty that lies within all in abundance.

Om Tat Sat

Preface

In a slender but significant work of rational faith, Barbara B. Pidgeon brings alive the universe of Rikhia, a *karmabhoomi* of Paramhansa Satyananda Saraswati and Swami Satsangi. Barbara brings to us the narrative voice of a seeker after truth: in many a reader-friendly way, she renders legible some profound and complex truths of yoga and *bhakti*. Of special importance is the last chapter where Satsangi gives her first interview concerning her life with Swamiji and at Rikhia from which we learn about the endless mission of Satyam (as I was privileged to call the Paramhansa).

Today, Rikhia is synonymous with Swami Satsangi, and underlying her sweet persona is a life of dedication to the Guru and the mission. In deft strokes, this work brings her persona alive for all, the initiates as well as laity. No one but Swami Satsangi could have completed Rikhia into the land of Satyam. The learned author's simple yet powerful statement compels: 'Behind Rikhia stands a story of enormous success and change. It is no longer the Rikhia that was "discovered" in 1989, a period that now seems like a distant past for the local community. And this has been achieved through the unwavering commitment, dedication and devotion of Swami Satsangi.' The transformation from abject poverty to collective self-reliance is the saga of Satyam and Satsangi.

That commitment led by Swami Satsangi's endless – and it remains important to stress – *non-violent* 'war' against patriarchy, even among the world's 'First Nations' peoples. Satyam and Satsangi constantly worked away against a patriarchal social order. And this work, even as it focuses on Swami Satsangi, offers a vignette of some worthy women saintly predecessors. Swami Satsangi leads, in exemplary ways, the work of women empowerment and gender justice.

This book is an unceasing elaboration of Satyam's own words: '*Perfect the unbroken awareness of your guru mantra with every breath and beat of the heart. This is your mission now.*'

Satsangi continues the mission and in the process transforms the lives of the sadly impoverished millions of scheduled tribes in and around Rikhia, and in building a world community of devotion and service for the 'wretched of the earth'. Expressed in terms of historic time rather than the timeless eternal, Swami Satsangi luminously follows the old even when ushering us into the new.

Dr Upendra Baxi   *24 April 2014*
Emeritus Professor of Law
University of Warwick and Delhi

Introduction

Life is a journey, a labyrinth of paths well trodden, sometimes a benign cycle of virtuous, enriching events, all too often a vicious cycle of disappointments and shattered dreams. Throughout the centuries, human beings have continued to live in similar patterns, repeating mistakes of the past over and over again. Our evolution has taken us technologically to a realm beyond our wildest imagining. Yet, emotionally, our basic, animal instincts all too readily come to the fore as we go on harming each other, and even ourselves, in the most unimaginably sophisticated ways. The First World War – and all the wars to follow – is a true testament to the ability of humankind to destroy one another with ever more efficient 'weapons of mass destruction', a term now common in our vocabularies. As supposedly superior and intelligent beings, we are not even emotionally developed to the point where most of us can adequately manage our basic of human needs; for example, the record numbers of illnesses attributed to our inability to even maintain a nutritional balance in our daily diets speaks volumes about us. A few people, however, throughout the ages have taken us by surprise by their positivity. They are role models that we can readily identify with but somehow cannot emulate.

In the tiny village of Rikhia in the eastern state of Jharkhand, India, there is a small group of people who have managed to succeed in controlling their emotional states of mind. Here are a few who have understood the futility of the lives that most of us currently lead. These brave souls were not satisfied with simply treading the same old paths that most of us tend to continuously do. A life of wish-fulfilling events, they realised, would not ultimately satisfy their need to understand life on a 'different level'. Quite unexpectedly in this remote area, this group of people has given up the repetitive journey of roller-coaster emotions. They have stopped the ever-running treadmill of life, stepping away to look within themselves and to serve others. They have chosen to live in a state of harmony and equanimity and, in so doing, are unselfishly also making an incredible difference in the lives of many impoverished, downtrodden people in this corner of rural India.

It is somewhat surreal to me that I find myself sitting today in Chennai, writing about a remarkable story of rejuvenation in a rural area in the east of India, a brief account about an extraordinary woman at the heart of these events. That I have had the most incredible privilege to meet and interact with this woman is quite astonishing to me.

I began my life in a small village in Scotland, my upbringing not extravagant by any stretch of imagination, but in a world far removed from the poverty-ridden rural, often forgotten, communities across the globe. Various events in my childhood, some traumatic, followed by a marriage in my teens and a divorce in my twenties saw me on my own with three very young children and no real clue about what to do next. Blessed with a sharp brain and a tough, determined character, however, I was able to turn these difficult circumstances to my advantage. Fiercely protective of my small family, only wishing them a better life than mine, I worked ceaselessly to create a professional career that has taken us on an incredible journey.

After some years, I found myself living in Muscat, my children by then university students, our Omani home their holiday refuge. I was working hard but loving the expatriate life, a beautiful home overlooking the Arabian Sea and an active calendar of social events. Physical fitness was a big feature of our lives, the searing summers not a deterrent to outdoor pursuits. Life was idyllic, a comfortable situation that I had no desire to change. Due to unforeseen events, however, quite suddenly one day, things began to change. After four hours of mountain biking in the searing heat of the afternoon desert sun, a regular and usually uneventful pursuit, I became severely dehydrated and ended the day in hospital, close to death. Recovered and relatively unperturbed, just two weeks later, while mountain biking again in the same terrain, a fall left me unable to stand without support and in acute pain. Quite literally and unexpectedly knocked out of my comfort zone, I began to question my life and whether I was really growing as a person.

I was having fun yes, my family was happy, but where was it all leading to? And it was then that I was introduced to Shiva, my *adi guru,* my first yoga master and the man who would help me to propel my life in different directions.

A Keralite, my newly acquired yoga instructor had been living in Muscat for a number of years before we met. I was one among a contingent of eager yoga students demanding his attention. But for me initially, and for some time onwards, he was one of the most infuriating men I had ever met. My remedial 'treatment' was to sit for twenty minutes a day watching my breath. Simple enough I thought, but as I attempted to put his instructions into practice, seemingly impossible. Pins and needles and agonising discomfort were the overriding sensations I felt. I regularly questioned him about the efficacy of this numbing practice. My complaints, however, fell on deaf ears as he more or less ignored me and advised me to get on with it. Somehow, despite my rising impatience and our regular quarrels, I managed to persevere with what seemed such a useless practice. Then at last, after one full year, I eventually mastered the task that I had been given. After what seemed like an age, I could actually sit comfortably for the allotted twenty minutes – the pain gradually and quietly subsided, finally slipping away, unnoticed.

During that year of mastering 'sitting', many aspects of my life started to shift for me, some changes too subtle to really pin down. I would go to parties and somehow not want to be there, staying for what I considered just long enough to avoid being impolite, gradually declining invitations altogether, giving some feeble excuse or another. I began to experience regular nightmares, unaware that they were most likely triggered by the practices that I had been assigned to do as suppressed emotions from the past began to emerge from my hitherto undisturbed subconscious mind. As I moved on through all the mixed experiences of this journey, I began to reflect more and more deeply on my circumstances and the person that I had become and, importantly, contemplating where this life would take me.

After three more years of practising yoga, I moved to Nigeria to continue my professional career, but by then I was also a part-time student of transpersonal psychology and consciousness. I conducted a couple of yoga sessions in my spare time also and was quite amazed to witness the changes I had felt within myself beginning to be brought about in others. Two years after arriving in Nigeria, I didn't have to think twice when asked if I would be willing to take up a new role in India. The seeds of yoga sown in me by Shiva had left me with a thirst to know more. No matter how many volumes of yogic philosophy I had read and pondered over, I realised that thus far I had only scratched a very tiny piece of the surface of this incredible science. I wasn't at all concerned about what I was being asked to do in the business sphere – I was confident enough to take on the challenge, do it in my own way and do it well.

Though the motivation for a move to India was not entirely driven by professional reasons, I knew that all my efforts would initially require to be focused in this direction. After some time, my new team in India became established and together we celebrated many professional successes together. 'My way' of doing things had changed considerably since the early days of my career. The yogic influences that I had experienced had equipped me to act in a more conscious way, doing the right things objectively rather than in an emotionally driven manner, but more intuitively adept. As this high-calibre group of people from across India became firmly established in their roles, after two years in India, my personal time was freed up, enabling me to begin my forays into the spiritual realms of India.

With a new yoga instructor and friend, I was introduced to a mysterious 'Sir' and, together, we had some encounters with saints living in graveyards and a 'lady saint' who could, apparently, simultaneously manifest herself in two discrete locations. A musician friend managed to get the two of us front row access to the famous hugging *amma,* a world-renowned 'guru mother' of India. I could go on to relate similar strange and wonderful experiences. But the most valuable moment for me during those five wonderful years in India was when I was introduced to Swami Satyasangananda (also called Swami Satsangi) by another yoga instructor and friend.

Since my early encounters with the world of yoga, questioning myself had considerably impacted my way of being. Over the years of my professional life as I sat in meetings with presidents, government ministers, boards of directors and so on in the many places that I lived in, I was now starting to admit to myself that while I was outwardly confident, there was always a questioning voice in my head asking why on earth these people ever listened to me. Inwardly, I had been nursing an inferiority complex, not really convinced that I was good enough; self-limiting thoughts had generally made me keen to please others rather than to do what was right for me. There was no doubt that I had progressed well in my career, but my true potential remained unrealised, buried deep within.

In virtually all societies, we are conditioned to the fact that men are the controllers of our lives. Men head the political scenarios across the globe, men direct the corporate sectors across the board and men are at the helm of the spiritual realms of life too. In such circumstances then, it is hardly surprising that I, and the majority of my contemporaries, are impacted by these 'norms' within which we grow. While intellectually, women can assert that they are just as capable as their male counterparts, it is a stark fact that the female psyche is predominantly governed by emotions. And, as a consequence of growing and developing throughout all our impressionable years in societies where male domination is the norm, the vast majority of us women are unable to rise above these internal notions of ourselves. Deep within, we see ourselves as subservient beings. We severely limit our own potential, our self-effacing emotional links to the past overriding our true intellectual capacity. The result is a pitiful loss to society and ourselves.

Swami Satyasangananda, the spiritual leader of the Bihar School of Yoga's Rikhiapeeth ashram in Rikhia, is one of the few women I have met who has a deeply felt understanding of her real worth, not held back by any self-limiting notions that readily tie others down. This remarkable woman has successfully realised her true potential to be a role model for women in all walks of life. She is the central driving force behind this small book.

I was introduced to her just a year before I decided to visit the Rikhiapeeth ashram in December 2011 to undertake a course in Kriya Yoga. Alone in my room in the evenings, I was totally absorbed in thoughts of writing about Swami Satyasangananda. I felt that it was important that more people were aware of who she was, what she had done and was continuing to do. We had met on just a few occasions, but in these moments I was so overawed in her presence that I usually struggled to think of something sensible to say, words that would not sound like mundane gibberish. But as absurd as these thoughts about writing her story were, they would not leave me.

But how, I pondered within the confines of my head, could I broach such a topic with this revered spiritual leader, a person whom I could barely summon the courage to say a few simple words to. How could I possibly be taken seriously, given that I was a complete outsider to the whole arena of ashrams and gurus and all the rituals that were a part of this mysterious world? But no matter how hard my rational mind argued to get rid of these thoughts, they would not leave me. And so, my rebellious and uncontrolled mind even resorted to attempts at sending ethereal messages to the Swami. Unsurprisingly, when it was time for me to leave the ashram in the chilly morning hours on 1 January 2012, there was no one standing there at the gates seeking to hold me back for discussions about my desired and seemingly bizarre writing mission. Off I went then with these crazy notions still firmly locked up in the crevices of my mind.

The conviction to take this forward, however, just would not leave me. On 24 January, I summoned up the courage to send an email to Swami Satyasangananda. After typical, but sincere, preliminaries the words were blurted out, 'During my time in Rikhia I thought about writing your biography, Swamiji.'

I was relieved to get this notion, so far not shared with anyone, out of my head. And once out, I was not expecting to hear anything more about it and for life to go on just as it had before my winter ashram visit. But, to my utter surprise, two months after I had summoned up the courage to send that email, on the Sunday morning of 25 March 2012, I received the following response: 'I was dwelling on the idea of your suggestion about writing a book on me. Well, after due consideration, I think that it can be done and the time is right for that.'

Incredulous at the possibility that my crazy notion could actually become a reality, I could only muster up a 'Wow!' in response.

When we next met in April that year, I was curious to understand why it was that Swami Satsangi had thought that I could write about her. The typical self-limiting and critical thoughts were bellowing loudly in my ears, insisting that this was a foolish idea that really could not hope to be fulfilled. I was moved and honoured, however, to hear her say, 'I believe that you were divinely inspired for this by Sri Swami Satyananda.'

And so my journey of learning more about this inspiring leader began. A journey that I came to realise would not be only about me knowing her, but one that would also become a search to know more about myself. And as I begin now to move on to this next phase in my own life, I move on with some certainty that:

> There is no permanence in the joy delivered from material gains... [we] are functioning with a mere fraction of the potential power of the brain... the higher faculties of the brain, which are latent, have to be illumined and awakened...

> Swami Satyasangananda Saraswati, 2003, p. 5

I am grateful to all the people I have met along the way in this phase of my life that is now coming to an end, and thankful, too, for all the trials and tribulations that gave me the inner strength to keep going. I remember, especially, the day that I sat in a friend's home nestled within the peaceful Palani hills of Kodaikanal, for that was where I retreated to write the first few words of what is before me now. And I will be forever thankful to a close friend who kindly spent many hours transcribing interviews, her sole motivation being the benefit she derived from hearing the beautiful voice of Swami Satsangi.

Most importantly, I am infinitely grateful to have been blessed with my family of Michael, Steven and Nicole, the three who gave me the impetus and the freedom to be where I am today. Were they not the model children that they came to be throughout their growing years, none of this would have been possible.

After twelve privileged years of wandering around the globe, I am about to return to London. I leave with the realisation that deep down, despite our many cultural differences, our societal norms of behaviour, underneath this thin veneer we are all essentially one, we can be at home anywhere we may wish to be... all we need to do is open up our hearts and set our true selves free.

A Silent Revolution

Swami Satyananda was a diminutive man, his physical frame just five feet two inches tall. But he was a giant of a man in what he achieved in his lifetime. No one even noticed his physical appearance for it was his energy, his insightfulness, his arresting words that were overawing and inspiring to all who had the good fortune to meet him. He walked the earth in this physical body for some eighty-six years, from 24 December 1923 to 5 December 2009, departing from the world at a time of his own choosing. His life's mission complete, he left just as he had entered, with no possessions of his own, just the few simple clothes which he wore in deference to the principle of modesty.

Swami Satyananda began his life by the foothills of the Himalayas in a small village near Almora in the north of India and it was there that he spent most of the first twenty years of his life before leaving his home, a young man, intent only on searching for his spiritual leader. He knew even then that life as an ordinary householder was certainly not his destiny. Shortly after embarking on this mission, he found his guru, Swami Sivananda, in Rishikesh, a city in the Garhwal Himalaya foothills renowned for its yoga centres. It was there that he spent most of the next twenty years of his life, a life of austerity as a disciple absolutely dedicated to his guru. When the time came to depart from Rishikesh, Swami Satyananda was mandated by his guru to 'Take yoga from shore to shore and door to door.' Through an exhausting schedule that entailed travelling extensively around the world, lighting the lamp of yoga in distant and often obscure locations and eventually establishing the Sivanandashram Bihar School of Yoga in Munger in the eastern state of Bihar, Swami Satyananda, without any shadow of a doubt, fulfilled the mission that had been entrusted to him. Over the twenty years that were to follow after pushing himself out of the comfort zone of his guru's ashram in Rishikesh, he founded, under the auspices of what is commonly referred to as the 'BSY', the Bihar School of Yoga, in 1963. Swami Satyananda established a world-revered institution with its core aim being to impart traditional yoga teachings to aspirants across the globe, with the ultimate goal to bring about a new way of being in world societies. The BSY provides traditional teachings in Yoga Health Management, Yoga Teacher Training, Yoga Sadhana, Kriya Yoga and many other programmes within the confines of very high-quality settings under the guidance of knowledgeable leaders. It hosts World Yoga Conventions attended by highly respected speakers in yogic sciences from around the world; conducts programmes in schools, hospitals, prisons, corporate organisations; ongoing research in the fields of medical science; and, not least of all, there are many programmes to support the underprivileged in society by providing a sustainable improved way of living. This list of activities is by no means definitive, these and many other activities clearly illustrate the wide reach and lasting benefits that the BSY has been instrumental in bringing about on a global basis.

Throughout his whole life, Swami Satyananda never personally owned anything of material worth, yet, when he departed from this earth he left behind a great legacy of achievements, the fruits of which are thriving well today. He left a legacy of accomplishments that very few have, or could ever hope to leave in memoriam. The main artery of the Satyananda legacy lives on at the Munger ashram and it is from there that the connections are maintained to the many institutions that grew from the seed that was planted there with Swami Satyananda's arrival in 1963.

Swami Satyananda departed from the Munger ashram in 1988, having some years earlier passed on the leader's mantle of this place to his foremost disciple, Swami Niranjan who was only twenty-three years old when he took on this role. Far from being an 'ordinary' disciple, Swami Niranjan had been entrusted to his guru's care when he was just four years old. Nineteen years later, as he took up the daunting role as the head of the revered Bihar School of Yoga, he was a man with vast experience in ashram and spiritual matters and well equipped to follow in the footsteps of his beloved guru. Swami Niranjan continues to be at the helm of this organisation, and it is under his leadership and guidance that the Satyananda legacy lives on to support the practitioners of this particular approach to yoga. Yoga centres of this school have been established, not just across India, but in countries all over the world, including Australia, Canada, Colombo, France, Greece, Poland, the United Kingdom and the United States – to name but a few. Swami Satyananda's teachings are perpetuated through these physical and corporate establishments which, in turn, are propped up by the wealth of books that he authored during his lifetime, the myriad recordings of his *satsang*s, his captivating discourses, and through a cadre of highly qualified, experienced teachers and spiritual leaders, a group of dedicated disciples all well equipped to continue his work. Millions of followers continue to learn and grow through the structured methods and practices of an integral approach to yoga, indeed to life.

Over sixty years of extreme hard work and self-imposed austerities, his single point of focus was to serve his guru and others, a lifetime's work any ordinary person would have been ready at this stage to retire from. And, for a short time, Swami Satyananda did in effect retire from this life of yoga and the infrastructure he had set up in Munger.

As the morning dawned on 8 August 1988 (8-8-88), Swami Satyananda left Munger, the ashram he had built up over the preceding twenty years or so. He walked out – empty-handed – to return to the relatively more carefree life of a wandering mendicant, in poverty and alone. He stepped out of the Munger ashram just as other wandering mendicants such as Saint Francis of Assisi or the Buddha had done so many years before him. Like him, they were also discontented with their comfortable lifestyles and leaving all they had behind them, they strode purposefully out in search for a deeper understanding of life and their place in it. So unattached was Swami Satyananda to everything amassed around him for the sole purpose of serving others that he simply told Swami Niranjan on that day in August, a day that that any ordinary person would have considered a tumultuous occasion, 'Namo Narayan. I am going.' Then, referring to the mission, the ashram he was leaving, he advised, 'If you are able to look after the work well, it will grow. If you are not able to look after it, let somebody else do it.'

And just like that, he was gone.

Swami Niranjan was left behind to fill the enormous shoes of his revered guru, he watched him leave, not once looking back. Swami Niranjan had already proved himself to be an extraordinary leader. Despite his young age, he was clearly competent to take on the role that his guru had handed down to him, but still, fulfilling the responsibility that was his destiny was a daunting task. He reflected some years later on what he considered his guru's most admirable quality:

> The quality that inspired me most... was his ability to always live as a disciple at heart. Externally he lived like a guru, but in his mind and heart he never considered himself to be a guru. He played a role for us, not himself. There was never any show of ego or any pompous air that he was a great man.

In his heart and mind he was never a great or learned man, he was always a seeker.

Swami Niranjanananda, 2008, p. 324

For a year, Swami Satyananda lived a mendicant's life, always remembering his *ishta devata,* the spiritual preceptor, Lord Mrityunjaya, whom he knew would guide him on what he needed to do next. His wandering came to an end when he arrived in the small village of Rikhia. Located in the eastern state of Jharkhand, Rikhia is a small village of Deoghar district.

At this point in Swami Satyananda's life – 1989 and his sixty-sixth year – there was a long and noteworthy list of accomplishments to his name. The relentless effort he had undergone in establishing a platform for yoga to be disseminated across the globe cannot be lauded enough, a science so badly needed in the stressful world in which we live today. But Swami Satyananda's real achievements, however, his most noteworthy efforts, can actually be found in the barely known, obscure and tiny Rikhia.

It was here in Rikhia that Swami Satyananda started what could only be described in hindsight as a revolution, a revolution that was set to bring about untold changes that would manifest slowly, stealthily but steadfastly and with sustainable outcomes. Rikhia would eventually emerge as a place that would come on the radar of the world map, a model of what can be done to bring about much-needed change in the world of stress and violence that we know today.

In 1989, this place was a forgotten and barren land, with

virtually no roads, no electricity, no easily accessible water supply. The place was inhabited mainly by the indigenous Santalis, their lifestyle an existence that had seen very little development for centuries gone by. Subsistence farmers mainly, their extended families were housed with a few goats and cattle in the small windowless huts that served as their homes. Education was almost non-existent, boys perhaps attending school sporadically for a few years, girls rarely making it past the first few grades – parents saw no point in educating minds that could only aspire to continuing the existence of their forefathers. While day-to-day tasks needed to be done, water to be hoisted from far-off wells, cow dung to be collected to fuel cooking of the evening meal or provide warmth in the winter nights, goats to be milked, an endless list of tedious tasks to be taken care of – where indeed was the time to continue a useless education. Yes, Rikhia and the district of Deoghar were so utterly dismal in those days, referred to as the 'darkest corner of the world' as one of the Swamis who was there in the early days recalled. She witnessed the malnourished children with their distended bellies, their small bodies so lacking in nutrients that even their hair was white, not the naturally beautiful black hair common to those of the Asian continent, their bodies barely covered by a few tattered rags. The doctor Swami, also there from the early days, remembered those suffering from many illnesses, tuberculosis prevalent among more than ninety per cent of the population, their weakened immune systems easily succumbing to this highly infectious and debilitating disease. In such conditions, even managing the few animals or farmland that some people had was a difficult chore; in fact, life itself would have been considered by many as a burden to be suffered through until its natural end, with no clue about how to change it, no understanding even of basic hygiene or maintaining a clean water supply for daily needs.

But go there today and you will see an entirely different situation – if you had seen the place in 1989 you would not be able to believe that it was the same place. Well-fed toddlers play along the still relatively quiet roadsides calling out 'Namo Narayan' to passersby, the greeting commonly used in the Rikhiapeeth ashram; older children ride their new bicycles to the now well-attended schools, smart school uniforms worn by all; well-nourished cows and goats meander across the fields, the village life buzzing with everyone playing their roles in allotted jobs, in the fields, at home or in the small tea and coffee shops built up around the area as meeting places.

So what happened?

Nothing short of a miracle, one must surmise. Rikhia was in an area that would certainly not have attracted the interest of any local, let alone national government bodies. Rikhia would not have been on the radar either of any NGO, non-governmental organisation, this place of no economic or global significance to any of the worldly powers at large. Rikhia was quite literally an area of no interest or consequence to anyone at all. What happened to Rikhia was the arrival of Swami Satyananda.

An unparalleled comparison perhaps, but with an imaginative mind we could compare what happened, indeed what is still happening in Rikhia, as similar to a conquest that would have been led by no less a person than the Roman Emperor Julius Caesar. Certainly, the wars waged by Caesar some two thousand years ago were undertaken with an entirely different approach and set of objectives, of course, but the significance was just as profound, albeit on a small scale. Just as Caesar lauded his victories with his famous words *'Veni, vidi, vici'* as he widened his vast empire into parts of Britain, so Swami Satyananda could rightly have declared that he came, he saw and he conquered. It was a conquest founded on love, as he conquered the negative vibrations that abounded in an area that had for centuries entangled all who had resided there into an endless, vicious circle of terrible hardship and misery. Gradually, the atmosphere changed, the tide turned and the downward spiralling life of squalor is now replaced with a palpably vibrant, virtuous circle, thriving with positive and energetic life. But this conquest, this revolution was a silent one. There was no banging of drums, no victory salutes, no modern-day media coverage. A series of positive changes were set in motion. Just as there was no outcry for help from these forgotten people in the past, silent victims in arduous times, there have been no cries of rejoicing either from the stoic population as their fortunes have been positively turned around.

However, as these changes in Rikhia begin to unfold towards positive consequences, the time is now right for these voices to be heard. At a time when the realisation is dawning across the globe that material wealth does not bring the peace of mind we seek, a lot can be learned from bringing the silent revolution that is Rikhia into the open. This is a revolution built on love and mutual respect across genders, old and young, the poor and poorer – everyone was given a voice and the opportunity to see their dignity and self-respect restored.

Finding Rikhia

But what was it that brought Swami Satyananda to the remote, little-known village called Rikhia? It would hardly seem to be a place where one would expect to find a guru of such enormous stature. Distinctly different in character from the more commonly known 'gurudoms' of Rishikesh and Varanasi, for example, it was also a far cry from Swami Satyananda's own well-established Munger ashram situated on the sacred banks of Ganga. Rikhia, till today, is not the easiest location to get to, though the journey there is hardly a deterrent for the countless number of people who regularly make the effort to go there. Most of the stalwart followers take the simplest route of a flight to Kolkata, trawling through that vibrant city to arrive among the masses thronging at Howrah railway station to then endure the train journey on the Janshatabdi Express to arrive six hours or so later at Jasidhi junction. Then they jostle through crowds before haggling for a reasonably priced auto-rickshaw ride to arrive at the point of destination another hour later.

On further investigation, however, Rikhia and the wider district of Deoghar were not always as obscure as one may think. Indeed, Mahatma Gandhi himself at some point had wanted to establish his own ashram in this area and, without doubt, he would have met Swami Satyananda's contemporary of the time, Sri Aurobindo, who was born in nearby Kolkata. No doubt, they would have discussed the furtherance of their mutual interest in the Indian movement for freedom from the British. Had circumstances been enacted out differently, Sri Aurobindo may have established his own ashram in Rikhia many years before Swami Satyananda's arrival, but as a vocal protestor against British rule in India, he was forced to flee the area to escape the British law-enforcers. It was to the French enclave of Pondicherry (now called Puducherry), the only place in India where he could be harboured in safety, that Aurobindo fled. Ironically perhaps, for the King's College, Cambridge graduate that he was, it was there that he resided for the remainder of his life, leaving his own legacy in the Aurobindo ashram and the well-known 'township' of Auroville in the outskirts of the city. The spirit of Deoghar, however, remained in Sri Aurobindo's heart, the area recalled by him in later years in his memoirs as a sacred environment, a memorable place that had a positive impact on his life.

Stepping out of the boundaries of the ashram walls that morning of 8 August 1988, Swami Satyananda left Munger with no particular destination in mind. Certainly, Rikhia would not have been at the forefront of his thoughts, its short-lived fame long forgotten. Rather, he put his unswerving faith in the cosmic forces with the absolute surety that he would be guided to his next resting place when the time was right – 'resting', of course, not the most appropriate word for this man renowned for the extreme efforts and exertions he made in his energetic life.

Without once looking back, Swami Satyananda strode out of Munger to embark on what was effectively a pilgrimage, travelling throughout much of the varied and vast Indian landscape and beyond.

> *Life is a pilgrimage.*
> *The wise man does not rest by the roadside inns.*
> *He marches direct to the illimitable domain of eternal bliss,*
> *his ultimate destination.*
>
> Swami Sivananda

Swami Satsangi, then a close disciple of Swami Satyananda, accompanied her guru throughout his journey during that year, she herself on a personal pilgrimage. Honoured to have the rare opportunity to spend time closely by her guru's side, she described their travels as *the most beautiful time of her life*, travelling throughout India with her Swamiji, from the Himalayas right down the west coast of India to Goa. It was a very different man that Swami Satsangi travelled with during this period. Until these moments they spent together, she had only seen Swami Satyananda constantly surrounded by large gatherings of devotees, always busy giving talks, guiding his many disciples, running the Munger ashram and the Bihar School of Yoga, travelling, being interviewed, writing.... Now he was free of this life, he had left these duties behind, an 'ordinary' man once again, for the time being anyway. Swami Satsangi saw that her guru was himself at heart a simple man, a devotee of his own guru as she was of him, the disciple that Swami Niranajan had known he truly was as had watched him walk away from Munger.

They were to visit many *tirthasthanas,* sacred places immortal gods like Lord Shiva, Lord Krishna and Sri Rama are said to have graced with their presence, divine places visited countless years before by saints such as *Adi Shankaracharya,* the eighth century yogic philosopher and scholar who restored the structure and practices from the ancient Vedic scriptures, and *Tulsidas,* the sixteenth century author of the *Ramcharitmanas* that so beautifully interprets the original Ramayana. Swami Satyananda and Swami Satsangi's journey took them to Kashi (Varanasi), the Vidyavasini temple, Allahabad, Kathmandu, Haridwar, Yamunotri, Gangotri, Kedarnath, Badri Vishal, the Vasukinath temple, Calcutta (Kolkata), Kalighat, Khajuraho, Ujjain, all of sacred significance.

Swami Satsangi was visiting these places of spiritual importance for the first time in her life. Although she had travelled all over the world, she was unaware about the many wonders of her own country, even visiting temples as if she was a foreigner in her own land. As they travelled, Swami Satyananda talked extensively about the places they traversed and stopped at. With his vast, exceptional knowledge, he explained details about the geography, the vegetation, the trees, the people, the language and so much more, regardless of which states of India they were in. He told Swami Satsangi that she had to be a keen observer in her journey, that she had to build a *samskara* for this land, a lasting impression of the holy sites and all that she encountered that would remain with her forever in her deep subconscious.

Swami Satyananda and Swami Satsangi visited Trayambakeshwar in the western state of Maharashtra. It is here, in the Shiva temple, where Lord Mrityunjaya, the dancing form of Lord Shiva, is said to reside. Lord Mrityunjaya was Swami Satyananda's *ishta devata,* his most beloved form of God, and it was to Lord Mrityunjaya that he had turned to in 1963 for guidance on what he should do in his life then. He made a devout promise then that he would return to him again when he had fulfilled his guru's mission and, having done so, he had indeed returned.

Swami Satyananda prepared to remain in Trayambakeshwar during *Chaturmas*, the four month period from July to October typically set aside in the Hindu calendar for austerities and spiritual observances, with the sole objective of determining what it was he needed to do in this next stage in the journey through this life. He had travelled for almost a full year, after clearing his life in Munger completely from his mind, and was ready to begin anew in a different direction. He settled in a room that was previously the *goshala,* the cowshed, a space just eight feet by eight but sufficient to meet his basic need of a sheltered place in which to sleep. He gave his watch and almost all that he had in his possession as an offering to the Lord. And then he began his routine life of daily rituals, drinking only milk twice a day and a very light evening meal, simply waiting for the guidance to come as he knew it would. Expressing his experience during this time, Swami Satyananda wrote:

14 July 1989

I am again at Trayambakeshwar, the *jyotirlinga* of Lord Shiva, after twenty-six years. It was here in 1963 that the chapter of my life which led me to Munger and the propagation of yoga was first revealed to me. It was here, too, that I made a *sankalpa* or promise to return and seek further enlightenment, renouncing all I achieve or accomplish for the propagation of yoga.

This morning I went to have *darshan* of Lord Mrityunjaya and sought his permission to spend two months of Chaturmas here. A strange coincidence brings me back to the same place after so many years. His Holiness Mahant Shivgiriji Maharaj, the chief of Juna Akhara at Trayambakeshwar, invited me to stay at Neel Parvat, the very same place where I had stayed twenty-six years ago. I have chosen to stay in a *goshala* at the foot of Neel Parvat, a small room 8 x 8, representing everything ancient in structure, purity and simplicity.

I am alone. What shall I do here? All around me rise the Brahmagiri hills from where the Godavari descends and flows on to the eastern sea. While I meditate under the Gular tree outside my *kutiya* and await his next command, I am inspired and intoxicated by the wondrous beauty of these Shiva-lingam-shaped mountains on all sides.

18 July 1989

Guru Poornima *vrat* [fast] begins today. At midnight I was bathing in the light when a cyclonic storm started and the command was clear:

'Perfect the unbroken awareness of your guru mantra with every breath and beat of the heart. This is your mission now.'

So here begins the new chapter of my life. And just as I gave my whole self to the accomplishment of His previous command, I shall also plunge deep into all that is required of me to perfect my new mission. The past is dead and gone. Human as I am, I may travel back into the past and circumstances may compel me to accept associations with those with whom I had interacted before. That too is His will, but my personal endeavour will be to break away from the past and fulfil the mission given to me by Lord Mrityunjaya.

Swami Satsangi met Swami Satyananda at Trayambakeshwar on 8 September 1989. She knew now what her guru would do in the next phase of his life but there was still the question of *where* to go. Swami Satyananda had spent most of his first twenty years growing up in his home town, often busy with the family farm; the next significant phase of his life was another twenty years or so learning from his guru in Rishikesh. He moved on from Rishikesh to fulfil his mission of taking yoga from shore to shore and door to door. And this was exactly as he did. For the next twenty years he travelled extensively in all continents of the world and many of his disciples established ashrams that still exist across the globe today along with the extensive home of the Bihar School of Yoga in Munger.

Then, aged sixty-five, the location for the next significant stage of Swami Satyananda's life had to be determined. Thirteen months after the day that Swami Satyananda had left Munger, Swami Satsangi was to hear first-hand that the important question of where Swami Satyananda's next phase of his life was to be played out would soon be answered.

8 September 1989

A question which has been haunting my mind from time to time is answered today. Where do I fulfil my next mission? Many places were offered to me – a beautiful cave at Gangotri on the banks of the Ganga, a *kutiya* at Kedarnath and many others, but I had reserved my decision until the direction was made clear to me. I woke up at midnight as usual. The sky was quiet; the translucent rays of Ashtami were shining through the small window of my *kutiya*, and I found that I was once again enveloped by a strange light. The command was clear:

'*Go to my burial ground, the* samshan bhoomi!'

That very morning, while I was boiling my tea, Swami Satyasangananda arrived all the way from Munger, and the first instruction I gave her was to find the place for me. I gave her a glimpse of what I had seen and described its setting and surrounding topography. She left barely three hours after her arrival, in search of the place of my description.

After hearing the vague descriptions of where her guru should now go, Swami Satsangi immediately left Trayambakeshwar. There was no time to lose on her mission to locate this place. In his vision, Swami Satyananda had had a glimpse of erect Shirish and Palash trees and the word *chitabhoomi,* burial ground, had flashed before him. He knew that the burial ground of Sati was in Deoghar and that was where he asked Swami Satsangi to begin her search for his next destination.

Though commencing her journey to locate the land with only this vague description of where she had to go, Swami Satsangi was confident of reaching her destination, her faith as strong as always in her guru's guidance. She took a taxi to Mumbai, a flight from Mumbai to Delhi, another flight from Delhi to Patna and finally reached Deoghar by rickshaw on 9 September.

When she arrived in Deoghar that morning, Swami Satsangi went to the temple with no particular purpose in mind other than to be in those sacred surroundings. The Baidyanath temple in Deoghar is a famous temple in India – one of the twelve Shiva *jyotirlingam* temples, always seething with people and deafening noise as everyone jostles their way along.

Swami Satsangi negotiated her way through the crowds all around her, everyone's senses heightened in the commotion and energy abounding in this magical place. Since it was her first visit to this holy temple, Swami Satsangi was desperately trying to take in all the sights, the sounds, the smells, the feelings and emotions while, at the same time, trying to avoid getting carried away in the crowds as everyone pushed and jostled to make their way to the core of the temple with the

Shiva lingam, the symbol that depicts the inert consciousness of God, at its centre.

Suddenly, through all the commotion, the temple bells, the chanting, police trying to keep order in the place... Swami Satsangi discerned an unusual sound. She was stopped in her tracks as she listened intently to what seemed to be a strange sort of laughter. Then she heard a voice, not a voice from the crowd, but a far-off voice, a voice that seemed to be coming from 'another dimension'.

For a few moments, time stood still. Then again she heard the voice and it was telling her that the next morning she would meet a man with three stripes, the distinctive markings made with ashes on the foreheads of followers of Lord Shiva; this tall and striking man would lead her to where she had to go. The voice that she was now hearing clearly told her that a snake would appear after she reached the correct spot.

It may have been just a few moments, but it seemed like a considerable stretch of time, when Swami Satsangi returned to her 'ordinary senses'. She was carried on in the flow of the crowd, but her mind was preoccupied with this strange experience as she finally emerged from the temple.

Later, back in her hotel for the evening, she could not get the strange 'conversation' out of her head. How, she wondered, would she be able to pick out one particular man with three stripes when around half of the population would have these symbols clearly displayed across their foreheads! And, from a personal perspective, she wondered about the snake and her fear of those creatures, which left her apprehensive.

The next morning, she left her room to start on her mission to locate the land. And quite unexpectedly, she immediately noticed a tall man standing at the entrance of her hotel, his looks striking, with light eyes, long hair, his body smeared with ashes from the ritual fires of worship in the typical fashion of the followers of Lord Shiva. Importantly, three stripes were streaked across his forehead. She stopped in her tracks quite flabbergasted at the sight of this man, looking at him, but not moving. He also noticed her and immediately walked towards her. He asked, 'You have come here for some reason?'

She replied that she was looking for some land for her guru. He then told her that he had a stretch of land, which he could show her, and she simply replied, 'Let's go.'

An astonishing set of circumstances were clearly unfolding, circumstances that many people may consider quite unbelievable. Not just the ethereal voice that spoke to her, but the mere fact that a young woman in India had gone on a mission, unaccompanied, to locate a remote piece of land was quite an extraordinary situation. And even though she had been given only vague instructions to complete her mission, she did so boldly, without any hesitation.

This is very much a factual account of what happened in these few short days – the world on our everyday level of consciousness is not all that there is to this life. And so it was that Swami Satsangi and the man she had only just met left from the hotel together. She travelling alone by auto-rickshaw, and he on his motorcycle, the convention of the time and location making it inappropriate for an unrelated man and a young woman to travel together in the same vehicle. They drove for what seemed an endless time – the land became more and more deserted as their journey continued, barren as far as the eye could see. A few kilometres later, they suddenly came to a stop. In front of them stood an old, crumbling house, a dilapidated well, a broken boundary wall, almost non-existent. Nothing else could be seen apart from some rubble in the silent place, which was entirely deserted.

On the 12 September 1989, Swami Satyananda wrote:

> It was on this day [more than forty years earlier] at Rishikesh by the banks of the Ganga, that my guru, Swami Sivanandaji, gave me Paramahansa *diksha* of the Dasnama Sannyasa Order.
>
> A swami from Munger arrived by mid-afternoon to inform me that barely two days after her departure, Swami Satsangi had located the exact setting in Lord Shiva's *samshan bhoomi* for my further mission. That evening I performed Poornahuti (final oblations) for the fulfilment of my prayers and the revelation of a divine place and a clear-cut path, just as BSY [Bihar School of Yoga] and Ganga Darshan had been revealed to me twenty-five years ago in the same place by the same Lord Mrityunjaya.

Swami Satsangi indeed had found the land – she categorically knew that the spot that she had been taken to was the one that she had been sent to find. Her emotions were mixed, however, partly with joy at having found the place that she had been looking for, but with a nagging fear in her mind about the possible meeting with a snake that had been told to her she would see. Certainly, the landscape was a likely one for such an encounter.

The man who, as the voice she heard in the temple had correctly predicted she would meet, had taken Swami Satsangi to the land was Giridhari Panda, the priest of the Harlajori temple in Deoghar. And it was he who assisted Swami Satsangi in getting the land registered on the very day that she was first taken to see it. Remarkably, all formalities were completed just three days later, possession of the land confirmed and duly handed over for a new purpose. The scene was then set for the next steps of her and her guru's intertwined lives along the paths that they were destined to tread together for some years to come. The fulfilment of Swami Satyananda's life mission was assured and another scene in the *lila*, the play of life, was set to unfold before them. At that moment, although deep down in her heart, Swami Satsangi was confident that she had done the right thing in buying this land, she was now overcome with misgivings wondering how on earth this piece of barren land could possibly be made habitable, the task to make it so, to say the least, quite daunting.

In May 2013, on the culmination of the Akshay Trithiya Puja held in Rikhia, I personally visited the Deoghar temple as I had done on a few occasions before. A priest guided me along the way through the usual jostling crowds, such as Swami Satsangi would have encountered, all intent on pushing their way through for a fleeting touch of the sacred lingam. As I looked into the priest's eyes, I realised somehow that he must be 'the one with the three stripes' who had initially guided Swami Satsangi to the *chitabhoomi* more than twenty years earlier.

He told me that, indeed, he was the same man and he was happy to recount his memories from that same momentous occasion. He told that me that although it was most unusual, unheard of, in fact, to find such a young woman all on her own in this remote location on such a nebulous mission, it all seemed quite natural. He knew well that this situation was one destined to happen, with him intended to play his part as ordained.

I heard also how this priest had remained connected with the events that had been unfolding since that day. And how he had been supported by Swami Satyananda to overcome any difficulties in his life throughout the years from that fortunate day when he had taken Swami Satsangi to find the land. Giridhari Panda was still a striking man, with unusually light and sparkling eyes, a learned man at peace with himself and his surroundings. He is a lifelong disciple of Swami Satyananda and still a regular visitor to the ashram, never missing the Thursday evening prayers in remembrance of his guru. I felt an immediate rapport with this priest who had been instrumental in the establishment of Rikhia. Asking him for his blessings, I felt an instant surge of energy flow from him to me. I was immensely grateful for our brief and fortunate encounter that day.

Swami Satsangi

S wami Satyananda was a prolific writer and speaker during his lifetime, leaving many books behind him when he departed this earth and many people who have written or spoken about him. Numerous recordings of the countless *satsang*s, his talks given at home and abroad, have been systematically and carefully archived to maintain access to a wealth of his profound insights on a diverse range of topics. The physical infrastructure of ashrams Swami Satyananda left behind also remain as a legacy, many of his followers equipped to continue to convey the many thoughts he carefully expostulated, messages most relevant for today's turbulent world. But there is relatively little known or written about the dedicated disciple who spent the last thirty years of her guru's life almost constantly by his side, the person who accompanied him on a large part of his pilgrimage after he left Munger, the person he sent to bring the vision he had of Rikhia to life and who he later entrusted the running of Rikhia to.

Swami Satyasangananda Saraswati, the *peethadhishwari*, the *acharya*, the preceptor and spiritual leader of the Rikhiapeeth ashram since its inception is, without a doubt, a remarkable woman as anyone fortunate enough to have met her can readily testify. Fondly referred to as Swami Satsangi, she was born in March 1953 in the small town of Chandernagore, just north of Kolkata in the state of West Bengal. In her twenties, she gave up a successful international career to answer an internally deafening call to move away from that life of material wealth, to follow instead a life of renunciation, to tread a path of search for the inner knowledge of her true being. In short, she chose the life of a *sannyasin*:

> *Sannyas* is not a mere ritual of abandoning one's garments and donning the saffron robes, or shaving one's head and changing one's name. It has a deeper and greater significance than that. It is the process whereby one abandons one's ego, one's desires, one's selfish motivation, one's hypocrisies and shames and, above all, one's limited nature. It is for this that the *sannyasin* disciple strives.
>
> Swami Satsangi, 2011, p. 49

Though her past life was a far cry from the traditional Indian life of rituals and temples, Swami Satsangi never looked back once her decision for this paradigm shift in her life had been made. She never doubted for a single second that this was the life that she was destined to follow. From the moment she entered the ashram she full-heartedly, fearlessly, steadfastly and earnestly deposited her whole being into this new beginning, a life certainly not for the faint-hearted renunciate who may have envisaged days filled with endless hours of silent meditation and pontificating. Daily life for all *sannyasins* alike necessitates periods of *seva*, selfless service, endless duties that need to be undertaken to ensure the smooth running of the ashram operations. The daily chores were many and varied from basic kitchen and cleaning tasks to building maintenance, stocking the library or editing and publishing documents, teaching yoga to the many visitors or simply cleaning the accommodation where they were housed. Swami Satsangi's long list of duties also effectively required her to act as a personal secretary to her beloved guru – not at all the lightest of her daily undertakings. Though many of the tasks she had to day may be considered menial and certainly not within the realm of her previous life, Swami Satsangi tirelessly undertook all that she had to do.

Not afforded the luxury of any solitude in the ashram's timetable, certainly not leading the life of a scholarly disciple, night after night Swami Satsangi stayed awake late into the early morning hours, intent on extending her limited knowledge of spiritual affairs. In an incredibly short period of time, she imbibed a prolific understanding of the complex texts of yogic philosophy. She soaked up the wisdom of the many great seers from thousands of years gone by, the great works collated in the *Puranas,* the Ramayana, the Vedas, the *Brahma Sutra*, the Bhagavad Gita and also the relatively modern-day postulations of Swami Sivananda, Swami Satyananda, Sri Aurobindo, Maharishi Ramana and so many others. In these early days she also undertook a formal course of study through the Open University on the teachings of Maharishi Mahesh Yogi, the renowned yogi known widely for his prolific teaching in transcendental meditation and regarded by many 'as the foremost scientist in the field of consciousness and the greatest teacher of our time' by the many institutions around the world that continue to spread the teachings he left behind.

Over a period of time, Swami Satsangi came to assimilate more and more of the vast and often disparate sources of information in the realms of yogic sciences. She became particularly interested in the obscure subject of *Tattwa Shuddhi,* a most complex *shuddhi* – a process of intense purification – of *Tattwa* – the very essence of our true human nature, in most of us veiled by the smog of our conditioned way of being. It is a beautiful process that allows us to get back to the pure human soul covered, in the majority of us, by the trappings of the material world. She kept coming across odd, fragmented pieces of information on this matter and, as she did, she became more and more absorbed in this ancient science. She began to encounter many strange experiences happening within herself as she progressed, often feeling that she was *somewhere else*, floating outside of her physical body. She wasn't just reading and understanding the subject of *Tattwa Shuddhi* on an intellectual level, she was awakening to the very primary substance of herself. It became clear to her that the information that had been uncovered by learned rishis and seers from the near and distant past, and now by her, was difficult to access, too difficult for any ordinary seeker to piece together into any usable format. Understanding this, and the potential benefits that could be garnered for others through gaining this knowledge, she incredibly, just two years after beginning her foray into an entirely different way of living, brought a comprehensive text on this complex subject to the public.

As we begin to understand a little of Swami Satsangi's capacity, we can appreciate how her achievements quite naturally led her to the position of the respected *acharya* of Rikhiapeeth. However, finding women in senior positions in the spiritual sphere of life is not typical. In fact, there is as much a dearth of women maintaining a relatively high status within this arena as in any other. The '*sannyasin* boardrooms' are just as bereft of women as their global business counterparts, the Europeans among them now attempting to implement legislation in this sphere to enforce a redressing of the currently male-skewed balance. The likelihood of such legislation in India, in any capacity, is a far-off dream and a situation that does not exist in the many male-dominated spiritual centres either. The vast majority of the current generations of women stand very little chance of being able to reach anywhere near their potential. Even today, many, many women are not even afforded a basic education.

So how is it that Swami Satsangi has managed to reach such an exalted position in this spiritual but male-dominated sphere? Against all the odds, how has she managed to attain, and for many years now retain, her undeniably elevated status? That she is a remarkable woman we have already understood, well deserving of the position she holds as the *acharya* of

Rikhiapeeth, the head of a flourishing ashram whose purpose is to 'Serve, Love and Give' in a spiritual, but non-secular, atmosphere. There are a few contemporaries of Swami Satsangi, past and present, whose lives we could compare to understand how a handful of women have managed to make their way to a similar status despite the same low odds.

Sri Anandamayi Ma

Another such remarkable female achiever in the spiritual realm is Sri Anandamayi Ma, a guru named by her followers as the 'blissful mother', most often referred to simply as 'Ma'. Ma was born in 1896 as Nirmala Sundari in the small town of Kheora, in what was then the West Bengal state of India, but post the 1905 partition, an area of Bangladesh. Unlike Swami Satsangi, Ma had little exposure to any formal education though her parents were relatively modern in their way of thinking. They lived during that era of Sri Aurobindo, Swami Sivananda, Swami Vivekananda, Sri Ramana and the many other spiritual leaders from the East who were regularly engaging in philosophical discussions and debates with their Western counterparts of the time, such as Carl Jung, Paul Brunton and Annie Besant, among many others. This was a time of considerable change as ideologies were shared and examined from new perspectives and standpoints. The young Nirmala was encouraged during this time to focus on her own spirituality and from childhood she had many esoteric experiences, evident to all around her. In accordance with the traditions of her culture, however, she was married off at a very young age, fortunately to an unusually understanding husband of those times, or even of today. He 'tolerantly' observed his young wife as she withdrew herself for countless hours of deep meditation, recognising that she was no ordinary, simple village woman but a self-enlightened being who spoke in depth of complex matters well beyond what would have been her expected intellectual capacity, given her limited exposure to any formal education or teaching. Her husband became her first disciple, soon followed by countless others, including one of her most well-known and ardent devotees – Jyotish Chandra Ray, a Bengali government official. Jyotish was totally enraptured by Ma from the very first time they met when he was in his mid-forties and he remained a devoted disciple until his last breath around thirteen years later, leaving some beautiful literature behind him in praise of the woman who had become his spiritual guide and guru.

Although clearly an 'accomplished guru' with a remarkably large following of devoted disciples, Ma never deviated from the cultural norms, the behaviour traditionally expected, enforced even, on an Indian wife. Despite her rising status in spiritual society and the reverence directed towards her day in and day out, despite the fact that she was establishing ashrams for her ever-growing number of disciples and opening schools for the underprivileged in her locale, she also remained a devoted, obedient wife, speaking only with her husband's approval, serving his food and generally taking care of his wellbeing. It was in this way that Ma ensured that she could express the spiritual side of her character, her otherworldliness, her ethereal being, without drawing undue criticism from the unofficial stalwarts who made it their personal duty to ensure societal norms were not breached. Ma never tried to fight against these constraints that may otherwise deter less determined souls. She chose instead to be a dutiful wife accepting these cultural constraints as her karma, her dharma, her undisputed duty; she had no egotistical problem in this regard and did not believe that she was compromising herself in any way at all. Ma encouraged others to do as she steadfastly did – by acquiescing to these societal enforced constraints of 'proper behaviour', she advised those that sought her guidance, they could also grow inwardly, quietly, without the fear of any negative consequences that may have arisen by any futile rebelliousness against age-old traditional norms. In this way, Ma was able to achieve all that she did and we can probably look back now and agree, that yes, for that time, despite all the modernisation and cultural exchanges, her quiet compliance to age-old traditions was the most appropriate behaviour for her to have adopted. Any other course of action would most likely have ended in a different set of outcomes.

The Mother

Madame Blanche Rachel Mirra Alfassa, another undoubtedly esteemed, spiritual woman leader, was born in 1878 in Paris, a child of Turkish and Egyptian immigrants of the Jewish faith. Like Ma, Mirra had several spiritual experiences from an early age, experiences at the age of five that led her, at that young age, to declare that she was not of this world. She was often found in trance-like states, an embarrassment to her mother who just could not comprehend what was unfolding in her daughter's life. In her early teens, Mirra described how she had regular 'out-of-body experiences', recounting experiences from past lives and firmly asserting that she had directly realised God's existence. Although these experiences were manifesting within her without any external connections to a physical guide or any exposure to relevant literature, by the time she was in her early twenties, Mirra had discovered Swami Vivekananda's Raja Yoga. Later on, an encounter with an Indian man she met in Paris led her to the Bhagavad Gita, inspiring her to continue in the pursuance of her otherworldly life. Mirra's experiences continued unabated as she actively interacted with many like-minded people caught up in the unparalleled world changes that were manifesting in this era of industrial and spiritual revolution, experiences that ultimately led her in 1914 to Sri Aurobindo in Pondicherry. Mirra immediately recognised Sri Aurobindo as the figure she often saw in her dreams, a figure she had understood until that moment to be that of Lord Krishna. So profound was his impact on her that she recorded the moment in her diary:

> It matters not if there are hundreds of beings plunged in densest ignorance. He whom we saw yesterday is on earth; his presence is enough to prove that a day will come when darkness shall be transformed into light, when Thy reign shall be indeed established upon earth.

Thus began a lifelong relationship between these two divine beings, the already revered Sri Aurobindo and the young Mirra, a relationship that culminated in the spiritual awakening of millions of followers, invoking the interest of people like John F. Kennedy and Henry Ford. It was a relationship that led to the opening of the International Centre of Education to provide a holistic approach to educating children in India; and the legacy of the world-famous town of Auroville together with a great raft of documented literary wisdom for the millions who still flock to the remaining ashrams in worship of the memory of Sri Aurobindo and his consort, the Divine Mother, as Mirra came to be called.

Other current-day contemporaries include Mata Amritanandamayi from the state of Kerala in southwest India, referred to by her millions of followers throughout the world as 'Amma', Mother, known for her selfless love and compassion towards all, her unique approach being to individually embrace each and every one of her followers who queue for hours to feel her touch, many of whom recount the inner transformation that follows their encounter with the 'hugging saint'. And so, too, in the West we see a few examples of women rising within the spiritual hierarchies there: Dr Ingrid Mattson, a professor of Islamic Studies in the United States and Ruth Messinger, president and executive director of the American Jewish World Service, as just two of the exemplary achievers. But overall, the numbers of such women in spiritual leadership positions is still a tiny minority, just like their corporate counterparts, a far cry from any state of equilibrium. And this situation prevails today despite a long history of verbal supporters of women's rights, men who advocated that women be considered on an equal basis to men, stretching all the way back in the history of time. They include influential figures such as the Buddha and Sri Adi Shankaracharya, Swami Vivekananda and Swami Sivananda and others we could go on to name.

So then returning to the question: how did Swami Satsangi and a few of her female contemporaries manage to reach to the heights that they did? To coin a phrase from Sister Maureen Fielder, the Catholic nun who has been described as 'a controversial activist within the Catholic church', how is it that these few, undeniably high achievers in spiritual realms, came to 'Break through the *stained* glass ceiling?' Why did these few women succeed in doing so and not countless others? All of them are accomplished achievers no doubt, but Swami Satsangi and her contemporaries are strikingly representative of the female population. Many of these women were 'self-realised.' Swami Satsangi herself lived the life of a *sannyas* in the *guru-shishya* tradition. The paths through which they arrived to their destinations, though, do not seem to be the attributable causes for their attained status; nor did they have to alter their true nature or discard their femininity, or pretend to be other than what they were. One just has to feel the warm embrace of Amma or listen to the beautiful voice of Swami Satsangi during one of her discourses as a testimony to this.

I believe that Swami Satsangi rose to her current status through her unwavering belief in her own capacity, her own intellect, drive, passion, love – her very own being. The difference in these women is that they have followed their hearts, their rightful paths and did not let any preconceived notion of false ceilings or any other limitations stand in their way.

> Our deepest fear is not that we are inadequate. Our deepest fear is that we are powerful beyond measure. It is our light, not our darkness that most frightens us. We ask ourselves, who am I to be brilliant, gorgeous, talented, fabulous? Actually, who are you not to be? You are a child of God. Your playing small does not serve the world. There is nothing enlightened about shrinking so that other people won't feel insecure around you. We are all meant to shine, as children do. We were born to make manifest the glory of God that is within us. It's not just in some of us; it's in everyone. And as we let our own light shine, we unconsciously give other people permission to do the same. As we are liberated from our own fear, our presence automatically liberates others.

Marianne Williamson, *A Return to Love: Reflections on the Principles of a Course in Miracles*

Gender Disparity

Swami Satyananda often discussed the fact that he had a close affinity with women, he 'knew them better than men' and recognised in general how women's capabilities differed from but complemented his own. He readily understood that in every culture across the entire globe, we could all testify to the fact that it is women who are the strength within the family unit. In difficult times, he witnessed how it was most often the women of the family, the mothers who quietly bore the suffering of others and did everything in their power to ensure that there was food on the table and a comfortable place to sleep in at night. It is the mother who carries her family's troubles within her heart and tries to see a safe way out. It is she who bears the child and it is she who, from that very first moment of her child's birth, holds an unbreakable bond of unconditional love no matter what circumstances arise in the times to come. He was acutely aware of the enduring affection that had been showered upon him by his own mother and how it was her guiding influence in his formative years that enabled him to grow into a tower of strength and a uniquely positive influence in the lives of many.

Swami Satyananda's belief in the endless courage of women, strengthened by his own mother's love, was also deeply influenced by a number of early spiritual experiences. As a young boy, for example, his parents were deeply concerned about their son's regular lapses into trance-like states and strange talk of visions that they did not understand. Intent on 'curing' him of these afflictions, they took him to see 'Ma' who most fortunately happened to be visiting their home town and they were confident that she would have a ready solution to resolve their concerns. However, as recounted by Sivarupa (a disciple of Swami Satyananda) in *Yogis of India*, Ma instantly recognised the boy as an 'elevated soul' and she merely showered her blessings upon him, urging his parents not to worry. For several days thereafter, the young Dharmendra (as Swami Satyananda was called then), remained in a sublime and blissful state. Although it was not the outcome intended by his caring parents, they were comforted nonetheless by Ma's unexpected declarations that their son was not, after all, suffering from some terrible affliction, in fact, rather the opposite was the truth.

Another early experience of Swami Satyananda's was with a learned *yogini*, a female yogi he unexpectedly came upon when he found her taking shelter on his family's land. His description of her was not flattering.

[T]otally illiterate and very ugly. Her body was as fat as a buffalo's and absolutely black like charcoal. She always smelled foul because she never cleaned her teeth, took a bath or changed her clothes. Her language was obscene and she would abuse anyone at the drop of a hat.

Swami Satyananda, 2006, p. 127

Yet he eagerly met this strange and unusual being on a number of occasions and it was this same yogini who initiated Swami Satyananda into Tantric Yoga, an ancient science that is a cornerstone and key differentiator of the BSY. This intense practice, not for the casual practitioner of yoga, can propel a serious yoga aspirant from his or her current level of evolution to a 'wholly different level of being' a transcendental level of deeply felt knowledge and awareness, a practice that was first described in dialogue between *Shiva,* cosmic consciousness, and *Shakti*, the cosmic energy. The understanding of this complex science has been sought by the early Westerners keen to explore the many facets of yogic practices.

Since the first Western explorer stumbled upon the science of tantra, scholars and laypersons have been vying to record their impressions on the subject. Thousands of books have been written, yet distortions are perceived as facts and hazy ideas abound. The reason is simple: tantra is not knowledge; it is experience, stimulated by the exchange with a master. Unless the experience comes, one cannot know tantra.

Swami Niranjanananda, 2013, p. ix

This yogini invoked Swami Satyananda's first transcendental experience, and it was on her advice that he embarked on a search that led him to find his guru, Swami Sivananda, in Rishikesh in 1943.

With such a high regard and deep respect for women, it pained Swami Satyananda to acknowledge that these same women are generally treated in society as 'somehow less' than their male counterparts. Women are considered inferior despite the knowledge in all our hearts and in our minds that there is no rational, logical or other basis for such discrimination. Yes, in some countries women are treated as equal to their 'other halves', but this is due to the enforcement of certain legal obligations rather than any shift in hearts and minds. In an even greater number of countries, however, there is either no legislation to support the women of our society to exist on a fair basis, or where it exists, there is limited or no enforcement of the supposedly instituted laws – at best, lip service is occasionally paid to any infringements. And most utterly confounding, it is a sad fact that in some countries there are even laws specifically enacted to severely limit the rights of women, to give official vent to the nonsensical notion that half of society should not be given a fair chance to flourish according to their capability.

The years that Swami Satyananda spent learning from his guru were in a very male-dominated society. Women, in fact, were not welcome to coexist in these austere ashram domains with their male counterparts. With his deep respect and love for his guru, he tolerated this imbalanced environment, recognising the limitations that worldly constraints can sometimes force one to accept. When the time came, however, for him to leave his guru's domain and the male-dominated system of which he had been an integral part, he could not forget his early experiences and he resolved not to perpetuate a way of life that supported the evident injustices of an unfairly dominated male-only world.

Swami Satyananda's understanding and belief in the powers of women were not founded on some superficial basis, not simply understood only on an intellectual level. His early observations of women were ingrained in his psyche and his personal quest to support the development of women came from a heartfelt truth that the natural order of the world required a balance. Just as we need a balance of night and day, dark and light, birth and death, we need also a balance of gender interaction just as the consciousness of Lord Shiva needed the energy of his consort Shakti to move from inaction into action. This was not merely empirical knowledge for Swami Satyananda, his personal experiences had made it quite clear to him how the natural balance of the world needed to be. He understood that the existing imbalance had far-reaching and scientific consequences, just as statistical data today provides evidence of the beneficial powers of a diverse body of decision-makers in the worldly sphere that determines our daily living conditions. These facts were not his only driving force to set things right, but as a man of absolute integrity and a man who firmly believed that any debt should be repaid, Swami Satyananda believed that he was indebted to the women who had been so influential in his life and was intent in ensuring that his debts were repaid.

Compelled to act on his inner convictions in an attempt to restore a natural equality in gender participation in the worldly and spiritual spheres within which he operated, Swami Satyananda personally supported and enabled women to reach their potential, not through token gestures and manipulation, but through recognising and nurturing potential. It is evident that it was not solely due to Swami Satsangi's belief in herself that she rose to the senior-most echelons of spiritual society. She would not even have been striving for such a position – her only aims were to know the truth of life and to serve her guru. She naturally took a leading role in the sleepy town of Rikhia when the ashram was being established, but it was Swami Satyananda who ensured that she was his successor. Subtly, throughout the years they spent together, he tried and tested her abilities and found in her someone who was a perfect fit for the role she would have to fulfil. In reality, nothing happened in Swami Satyananda's life by any chance or random set of events – all of his actions and his interactions were performed with clear intentions.

Throughout his life, Swami Satyananda was one of the very few men to take any serious interest in the plight of women. Many other men have, as we all know, discussed this topic, saying that this destructive disparity in our societies must be redressed. Swami Vivekananda was one such man. This most revered monk who took the world by storm as he captivated audiences across the world, most notably in Chicago as he addressed the

World's Parliament of Religions on 11 September 1893, calling for universal tolerance and peace. He declared: 'If there is any being I love in the world, it is my mother... The love which my mother gave to me has made me what I am, and I owe a debt to her that I cannot repay.' But yet he did little, if anything at all, to change the lot of women during his lifetime. And many other men, too, have made similar statements, but they did not really translate these words into any meaningful action. Swami Satyananda, however, continuously took affirmative action to change the plight of women in society. He worked hard to redress such imbalances and the detrimental consequences he witnessed all around him. He saw this situation as the root cause of disharmony in the world and was prepared to actually act, to do something about it.

Swami Satyananda found the right time and the right ingredients to act during his mission. When Swami Satsangi first entered ashram life, Swami Satyananda clearly told her then that she was required for 'his future mission'. She had no idea then what it was nor what her role in it may be.

It was not at all by chance that Swami Satsangi became, and continues to be, at the helm of the Rikhia ashram. Swami Satyananda knew that to make an impact in correcting the gender imbalance, he needed a strong and courageous woman by his side. He realised that only an energy such as Shakti in its manifested form could ever bring about a deep-rooted change. He knew the seeds to bring this to fruition would be firmly and carefully planted only by a person with the characteristics of Swami Satsangi.

Rikhia Beginnings

By 15 September 1989, shortly after the 'discovery' of Rikhia, the 'deal' was completed and the land was in Swami Satsangi's hands. She was joined there, in this 'burial ground' described in Swami Satyananda's vision just a few days earlier, by a couple of Swamis from the Munger ashram. Together, this small group of dedicated disciples determinedly began to bring the remote and barren place to life.

The district of Deoghar, in which Rikhia is situated, is no ordinary burial ground, however. There is a beautiful love story about Lord Shiva who, distraught at the death of his consort Sati, or Shakti, carried her body in his arms while performing the *tandava nritya*, the celestial dance of destruction, wreaking havoc in his wake as he traversed the universe in a rage. His dance compelled Lord Vishnu, preserver of the universe, to intervene and restore peace. Consequently, Sati's body began to disintegrate and fell in pieces over sixty-four locations across ancient India, an area more vast than present-day India. All of these sixty-four places, or Shaktipeeths, are said to be seats of cosmic energy, radiating vibrant waves of highly evolved energy fields that confer blessings on all according to their hearts' desires. Consequently, these locations are all considered to be sacred pilgrimage sites of Shakti worship – not quite burial grounds of our worldly experience, but rather, places that witnessed great outpourings of emotion between two sacred beings.

Sati's 'heart', it is said, had fallen in Deoghar, making this location of particular interest to devotees of Lord Shiva, a site that saw the concluding chapter of a beautiful love story, the ending of a display of absolute, unconditional love and devotion. These 'Shaivites' go to extreme lengths to visit this place to obtain the *darshan,* the blessings of their beloved Lord amidst the wonderful vibrations and energy evidently felt there. Throughout the year, and in particular during the months of July and August, in the searing heat, devotees walk barefoot from the Baidyanath Dham temple of Sultanganj in Munger to the Deoghar temple. A distance of around 100 kilometres needs to be covered, along paths that could hardly be termed as smooth terrain, to reach the destination. Walking night and day along these rough and dusty roads in the summer months is a challenge most of us would not even contemplate embarking on. And roads are not the only obstacle for these devotees – many other austerities also have to be observed, carrying heavy pots of sacred water from the Ganga along the way with them just one other example. Yet, two to three million people complete this journey every year, ecstatically pouring out the protected pots of holy water along with their devotion as offering to their beloved Lord once they reach their final destination, all the painful experiences quickly forgotten.

But, sacred as this area was, the stark fact remained that the plot of land on the outskirts of the temple, was still empty and barren. As Swami Satsangi and the small group came together to survey this totally desolate place, they did not have any clear idea of what they needed to do or where they should begin. It was starkly bare, with just the few trees that Swami Satyananda had described in the vision. This tiny army, nevertheless, was quite undaunted by the mammoth task of making the place habitable. Strengthened by their unswerving faith in their guru, these disciples had seen how he had transformed the area where the Munger ashram still stands, how he had made his mark across India and the globe, how he had also changed them. They had complete faith that they would soon see the metamorphosis delivered. And so they set about their task, comforted to an extent by the relatively favourable climate of Rikhia, situated as it is on a high plateau where the air is dry and even on the hottest days is cooled by a breeze, unlike the sweltering, still days of a summer in Munger.

When Swami Satsangi recounted these early days at Rikhia, she recalled how she had not even seen a well in her life before then and how she had to have the dilapidated well at the site cleaned up and a pump installed to ensure their basic need of a water supply was met. An electricity supply had to be arranged and basic toilet facilities constructed. Everything they needed had to be brought from Deoghar, whether it was nails, plastic, screws, bricks, sand, or cement – 'everything under the sun', managing these logistical complications on their own a difficult enough task from this isolated location.

Swami Satsangi, not surprisingly, aroused the interest of the local villagers in the vicinity. She could be seen working endlessly throughout the days and nights; driving tractors to plough the land, constructing walls with bricks she herself made, digging holes, laying cables – unimaginable tasks that this rural community had never seen women undertake before. These neighbours were naturally curious about the strange happenings around them. They were certainly unaware, as even Swami Satsangi herself would have been then, of the extent of the impending change that was to come.

Change would be brought about, as we will see, not just on the physical level, but on the ethereal, the very being of the place. Rikhia was a rural area inhabited mainly by subsistence farmers who barely managed to get by on a day-to-day basis, living from moment to moment. These same people were ready to work as labourers, keen to add to their meagre income and ready to assist in the onerous task of turning this barren land to a habitable one. Mustering together the largely inexperienced crew of Swamis and the somewhat bemused local workforce, this small group set out on a mission to get the place ready for Swami Satyananda's imminent arrival.

The local labourers were paid on a daily basis, their lifestyle such that their unexpected 'windfall' on one day meant that they often did not return to work the following day. So many frustrations were encountered at the time, perhaps least of all that the group of Swamis and the local workforce did not share a common language. But somehow they managed their way through all these difficulties, this small team of Rikhia pioneers joining together in their efforts for their common objective. They were lucky to find a man from Rikhia who took control of the labour and materials, even ensuring there was cooked food for their evening sustenance, a most welcome supply of rotis and dal.

At midday on 23 September, Swami Satyananda arrived in Rikhia. It was the day of the autumn equinox, one of the two days in the year when day and night are equal, falling in Western astrology in the month of Libra, depicted by the symbol of equally balanced scales. It is a day also of esoteric significance for a spiritual aspirant who must necessarily journey through the dark side of his soul where transformation takes place before light can truly enter into the depths of his heart. Swami Satyananda, as previously said, never did anything by chance, events in his life were never mere coincidences, strokes of luck or some misfortune. And it was certainly not just a coincidence that he had arrived in Rikhia on that day to begin the last chapter of his journey.

Swami Satyananda knew he had reached his rightful destination – Rikhia was without doubt the place he had seen in his vision on 12 September, just eleven days earlier. Instantly, he was at ease in this place, the pervading atmosphere buzzing with energy but also imbued with tranquillity, a graceful beauty. Only one week had passed since the arrival of the disciples at their new abode, but Swami Satyananda could see a place with a surrounding boundary wall, a gate through which he had to enter, a functioning well with a bountiful supply of water, an electricity supply for basic lighting, a small but adequate kitchen for the preparation of simple food, makeshift toilets and some tented accommodation. Exhausted but quite elated by what they had managed to achieve in such a short space of time and despite all the challenges that were encountered, Swami Satsangi and her fellow Swamis were ready with open arms to welcome their guru. Little time was wasted in exchanging pleasantries, however, as Swami Satyananda, a man with a divine mission, took control and quickly started to dictate to Swami Satsangi the long list of tasks that needed to be done. A somewhat relieved Swami Satsangi was delighted to be back in her assistant role – she is a woman of immense stamina and abilities, but above all else, always a loving disciple dedicated to serving her guru.

Swami Satsangi's good fortune had led her to the priest, Giridhari Panda, who had taken her to the land. Events had been unfolding as was foretold to her in the Deoghar temple. It was also indicated to Swami Satsangi that there would be a snake at this place, but to Swami Satsangi's relief, there had been no such manifestation thus far.

On the very day of Swami Satyananda's arrival, however, this revelation came true. The disciples were amazed by an extraordinary and unexpected sight – a large *geru* (orange) snake, about twelve feet long and six inches wide. They watched, incredulous, as the strange serpent completed three circumambulations of the property, as a devotee may complete his 'rounds' in the temple. Time appeared to stand still for those few moments, then just as quickly it had appeared, it vanished with lightning speed back under the tree from where it had emerged. Somewhat stunned, they searched for it around the tree, but there was no trace of the snake. The spot from which the snake had emerged was then marked to commemorate the event. Later, as they considered the spectacle that they had witnessed, Swami Satyananda informed them that this was an event of some considerable significance. The snake is a recurrent feature in Hindu and yogic philosophy. It adorns Lord Shiva's neck and body as well as the many manifestations of God in India although the ever-present snakes on the many forms of Shiva have their own significance. The snake is coiled three times around Lord Shiva's neck, the Lord of seemingly contradictory opposites, both the Lord of creation and the Lord of destruction, symbolising how he transcends the cycles of creation and time – past, present and future.

The snake's brief appearance, Swami Satyananda asserted, was a *darshan*, a blessing, from Lord Shiva himself. The snake had seemingly disappeared before their eyes into the core of the earth, just as Swami Satyananda would journey over the coming months and years to the very core of his being also to transcend the worldly dimensions of time, space and causation. This spot was an important landmark, auspiciously pointed out by the *geru*-coloured snake, destined to be the exact location for Swami Satyananda's future *sadhana*, the practice in his spiritual journey that he had come specifically to Rikhia to undertake.

Still, there was much work to be done before the Rikhia site was fully ready to house its new dwellers. They had to work to get the place ready for the guru Swami Satyananda, a seeker who had already achieved so much on his spiritual journey, but still to venture much further along this path than any ordinary person could even consider a possibility, a path that required immense courage, strength and conviction to follow.

Over a relatively short period of time, the local community got used to their new neighbours and work continued unabated. Swami Satsangi was heard from time to time giving the builders loud and piercing orders, asking, 'Do you want to work or not? If you do not want to work then go away. We have not engaged you to give away forty rupees every day!'

Despite the arguments every day, Swami Satsangi knew each of the builders by name and over time, a strong mutual respect developed. The builders were Santalis, a tribe of about six million people with their own culture, traditions and language. The Santalis live in the eastern areas of India, such as Jharkhand, Assam and Bihar as well as in Bangladesh, Nepal and Bhutan. They are most typically agriculturists and labourers, renowned for their honesty and a strong work ethic. Such was the respect for these people who had joined together with Swami Satyananda and his disciples in the making of Rikhia, that they were referred to as *vishwakarmas*, the divine builders. All of the masons, the electricians, carpenters, plumbers or horticulturists needed to build the ashram were locals. The degree of sophistication in the work included even the drainage system, which was built to enable collection of waste in underground pools for recycling. To establish such a close cooperation at any building site anywhere in the world is quite a feat, but especially for a young woman in a deeply conservative area of India, where women are typically considered inferior by their male counterparts.

While the foundations of the developing ashram were being constructed and trees planted, the foundations of many long and lasting relationships were also being laid. There was an old man called Narayana, for example, from the nearby village of Amarwa. He was asked to maintain a secure system of entry through the ashram boundary walls. Illiterate, but, as Swami Satyananda described him, a gentleman and a man with a high regard for Swami Satsangi as he witnessed first-hand all that this remarkable woman was able to accomplish.

By July 1990, the site at Rikhia was ready for Swami Satyananda to commence his *sadhana*. Sri Panchadashnam Paramhansa Alakh Bara was the name given to this particular site that was to be his *tapobhumi,* the name given to a place where a yogi can undertake his or her intense practices without disturbance, and the place, in this case, where Swami Satyananda intended to make his isolated home for several years to come.

Before Swami Satyananda embarked on this next stage of his divine life, he gave an informal *satsang*, a discourse on what he now intended to do:

> *Alakh* means 'freedom' from any kind of karmic bondage, and like *moksha*, *nirvana* or realisation, it is just a different name for the same thing.

The body is made strong like a *vajra* (the thunderbolt of Indra) through *sadhana* – nothing can break it; nothing can influence it. In the summer there is a *sadhana*, to endure heat. The body should not be affected by heat. The natural system of air-conditioning in the body begins to function.

In the winter, the *sadhana* is on freezing cold winter days, to spend your full day in the middle of a freezing cold river. Your physical endurance must grow, and along with that physical endurance there is a mental and psychic endurance also.

Inside the Alakh Bara, through *sadhana*, you come down to the nitty gritty, and once this happens, the grip of fear is no more, the grip of sleep is no more.

Instead, one experiences a perpetual state of consciousness totally absorbed in itself. There is no fluctuation between internal and external; between light and darkness. The body sustains itself, changes and becomes divine. It transforms and begins to derive nourishment from everything in its surroundings, nourishment from the *prana*.

Swami Satyananda made it clear to all his disciples that until and unless he was guided by his *ishta devata* to do otherwise, he would remain in isolation, dead to all his past associates, reverting from the guru back to the disciple treading the path towards his goal. And so Swami Satyananda, with these clear and strong messages delivered to his followers, embarked on this next phase of his life. From then, most of his time was to be spent outside in the open environment, a simple, basic life, except for the use of a *kutir*, a small hut with a thatched roof built for his use, the only building that Swami Satyananda would spend any time inside for the next several years while he performed his austere *sadhana*. During the summer months in *Panchagni sadhana*, *pancha* meaning five and *agni* fire, he would undertake this spiritual practice with four fires burning all around him under the hot sun, the fifth fire, blazing overhead. This not enough, however, to accomplish what he set out to do – in winter he had cold baths outside by the light of the moon and the stars, sitting for hours thereafter in *pranayama* practice. These complex rituals that had to be performed in strict adherence to ancient principles are not at all, of course, for any ordinary being. Such *sadhana,* spiritual practices, as these were only passed on from guru to disciple, to deserving *sadhaka*s as had been the tradition for many, many years in the Shankaracharya lineage. Swami Satyananda, with his immense strength and courage, undertook his mission with total devotion as he had promised.

Om Namo Narayana

O Lord Mrityunjaya.

I have worshipped you

as Kaal Bhairava with one,

as Kaamakshi with flowers, fruits, water and milk.

In many forms, in many ways

and in many places

I have worshipped whatever form

you have revealed to me as your own image.

And now, at your burial ground

I will worship you with every breath.

This I promise.

Swami Satyananda

Neighbours' Needs

Life never stood still while Swami Satyananda undertook his personal *sadhana*, his austere quest to even more fully and deeply know and feel the meaning of his life. The Rikhia neighbours had seen others come and go in the fleeting past – Mahatma Gandhi, Sri Aurobindo just two of the famous personalities who had momentarily been in their midst, but not long enough to leave any lasting impressions. But over time, there was a sense that this small group of Swamis now amongst them were there to stay, and, as the steadfast relationships began to build up from the early days of their new neighbours' presence, their lives began to be enriched and flourish.

As mentioned earlier, Narayana, the gentleman who was responsible for guarding the boundary walls, had developed a high regard for Swami Satsangi and he invited her to his home one day. Gracefully accepting the invitation, she went to meet him and his family in their nearby village home. She had met many local people but this was the first time that she would visit one of their homes. She was not prepared, however, for what she saw there. Home for her friend Narayana, a man who used to recount his memories of the First World War, was a small, dilapidated hut, one small room, no windows, no basic facilities, just bare walls, bare floors and the barest of essentials. Yet this space accommodated the entire family of husband and wife, son and daughter-in-law, daughter and grandchildren and, not to be left out, the few goats and chickens they owned – all crowded under one tiny roof. Although a common way of living for millions in India, this was not the India of Swami Satsangi's experience, not the memories she shared from her largely forgotten childhood days of a relatively privileged upbringing.

Returning to the ashram after this visit, Swami Satsangi reflected on the distant recollections of her own early days in the French enclave of Chandernagore where she had been born. She enjoyed a 'normal childhood' one would say, born to loving parents, the youngest in a family of four boys and two girls. Her family lived in fairly comfortable circumstances, enjoying life in a carefree manner as is the norm of the middle and upper classes of India who lead comfortable lives with domestic staff to take care of all of the mundane household chores. As the youngest in a family of six children, undoubtedly she was a bit spoiled, allowed the luxurious opportunities to pursue her personal desires.

Just as was the case in the French enclave of Pondicherry, the colonial rulers of Chandernagore did not just pack up and leave on India's independence from colonialist rule. Many of the 'infiltrators' remained in this place that had become their home, many French customs and the language, their ways of living and their presence continued being an influence on the lives of people living there.

Swami Satsangi attended a convent school run by nuns, a school that was attended by students of several nationalities. Consequently, in her early life, she was also exposed to many different cultures and religions and, importantly, she had ample opportunity to interact with her peers in a relatively relaxed environment. Typical of any young girl growing up in any part of the world, she enjoyed the company of her friends and the social aspects of school – she enjoyed drama, played basketball and other sports and generally felt unrestricted in pursuing her interests. It was within this atmosphere that Swami Satsangi excelled at school to the extent that she was taught with peers two years older than herself and consequently, she was academically ready for university at the young age of fourteen.

For a girl in any country, leaving home at such an early age is unusual. But for a young woman in India, particularly at the time in which Swami Satsangi was growing up, going to university itself was unusual, but going outside one's home and at such a young age would have been quite unheard of. Swami Satsangi's parents had the courage and conviction to allow their daughter to leave home to study at the University of Delhi – clearly, her parents must have trusted their daughter's abilities and good judgement to allow her to proceed as she did.

Swami Satsangi was an extremely happy young woman, well aware of her good fortune in having such liberal parents.

One year after graduating from the convent school in Chandernagore, she left home for Delhi University to take up a course of study in English literature, an academic life, but one that also allowed her to follow her interest in drama and the arts.

Swami Satsangi's memories of her childhood days are ones of absolute joy. In her words:

> School life was quite beautiful in the sense that I was making friends, acting in school dramas, listening to and playing music, singing and dancing. I also thoroughly enjoyed sports and played basketball. All what may be termed the extra-curricular aspects of school I enjoyed immensely. Studies, though I did well in them, I could have happily missed.
>
> After school I went to university in Delhi where I studied English literature and this I enjoyed a lot. But I was still able to make time for drama and sports as I had done at school.
>
> All in all, my years of study were quite blissful, I really didn't have a single worry in the world.

Coming back from her reflections of the past after her visit to Narayana's home, Swami Satsangi was somewhat distraught at what she had witnessed of her neighbour's plight, the family's impoverished life was such a far off comparison from her own young days.

Swami Satsangi was mindful of the fact that she was in Rikhia for one purpose only. She was there solely as the dedicated disciple of her beloved guru and her role was to ensure that Swami Satyananda could remain in total seclusion in the furtherance of the completion of the *sankalpa*, the resolve that he had undertaken to pursue his personal *sadhana*. She alone had been entrusted with this task and she knew that first and foremost that was what she had to do.

Yet Swami Satsangi made her own *sankalpa* – she resolved to work to improve conditions in the area that was now her home. When the opportunity arose to discuss her dilemma with Swami Satyananda, he was not surprised to learn of the local circumstances. Not complacent either, he encouraged Swami Satsangi to do the best that she could do to help these people.

Gradually, the circumstances of people in Rikhia began to change. But, just as all actions under the auspices of Swami Satyananda proceeded, the initial quest to support these neighbours did not begin in a haphazard way. Quite used to undertaking any plan in an organised manner, Swami Satsangi realised that they could not just go out and undertake random acts. She realised that they had to understand the most pressing needs of this rural community, this not an easy task in itself since there was no readily available data of local demographics. So the first thing she did was to personally set out to commence the recording of vitally important data about the local community, numbers of people, ages, gender, state of health, sources of income, etc. Joined by the other Swamis and the doctor on board, they eventually obtained a comprehensive overview of information, a vast improvement on the largely non-existent government records, to assist them in determining the population's most urgent needs.

Support began with targeted and structured construction of

some houses, so that the living conditions of some people were slightly uplifted. A few auto-rickshaws and carts were provided to enable others to earn their own incomes. Clothes came next, along with some basic items for women and children, the old and the sick. The Swamis residing in Rikhia would often go to the villages with their supplies. Singing *kirtans*, the villagers would gather around them and in the festive atmosphere, offerings were distributed to all. It took time to put these measures in place, but these gestures could only amount to small chips in this vast cavern of abject poverty, little dents around the edges of these rural villagers' lives, touching the lucky few. They were not yet sustainable actions for the long-term and continuous upliftment of the entire community. All these efforts were undertaken with the very best of intentions of course, but amounted really only to charity. Swami Satsangi had to concede it was not the way for effective development in the lives of their neighbouring communities, no matter how systematic the approach adopted was.

When Swami Satyananda arrived in Rikhia, he had made a *sankalpa* to repeat his mantra 10,800,000 times, or 108 crore times. The number 108 has its own significance in yogic science that we won't discuss here – suffice to say for now that this was not a random number but rather, as in all matters in Swami Satyananda's measured path of transformation, a number of importance. And, as anyone will know who has tried for themselves, concentrating fully on only one *mala*, string of beads, 108 repetitions of a mantra is in itself a difficult task, since the mind continuously wanders aimlessly away to consider other matters. The attention is abruptly brought back to the mantra only to wander off again and again and again. Indeed, Swami Satyananda had a considerable feat to complete. But after ten hours a day for three hundred days, he had completed this part of his arduous task.

As this period of Swami Satyananda's *sadhana* was coming to fruition, he received a divine message that determined which direction he must go towards next. Just as he had received the message of where to go to undertake this intense and important practice that was coming to an end, he clearly heard a voice telling him what his next course of action should be. This inner conviction was telling him that he now needed to turn his attention to helping his neighbours, the local villagers. The directive was given that he should love his neighbours, he had to ensure that, just as he had been provided with a place to live and food to eat in his life, so also they should have these basic needs met with his support.

From the very moment Swami Satyananda received this message, the quiet, sleepy ambience of Rikhia was set to change. With profound empathy for those around him and a renewed vigour from the strenuous tasks he had just endured, he made ready to get into a period of sustained activity. He well understood his own guru's directive to 'serve, love and give' and this period of isolation and intense practice had strengthened his resolve to carry his mandate out to the end. He stated:

> Service is the greatest purifier of karmas and without internal purity life is meaningless. It is through service that spiritual

evolution gains momentum and the inner journey towards
the highest knowledge begins.

And so a more rigorously structured approach and plan of
action started to emerge through the joint forces of Swami
Satyananda, Swami Satsangi and Swami Vedananda, one of the
Swamis who had joined the Rikhia pioneers from the Munger
ashram. As they worked together for the betterment of all in
the locality, help poured in from many directions. Cows, for
example, were donated through Swami Janakananda from
Denmark; when Swami Niranjan returned from a European
tour, he brought news of animal donations from various sources
there and many more such practical and generous contributions
were offered. Such donations were of the utmost practical
use for the local community of agriculturists and subsistence
farmers. At a convention in Munger, people began to hear about
the work of Swami Satsangi and the group of other Swamis
at Rikhia. Without any prompting, truckloads of clothes,
blankets and many other essential items began to arrive. As
all these donations came flooding in their distribution had to
be carefully managed, and this was worked out in an efficient,
equitable manner in close collaboration with the village leaders.
Together, the ashram-dwellers and the villagers embarked on a
structured approach to building houses for the people too, thus
deriving a multitude of benefits for all, not just in the shelter
provided, but from the wages earned by those involved in the
construction. As these local people, in turn, were spending
their newly generated income, so also, natural entrepreneurial

tendencies began to come to the fore in the local community. Not only did the new wage-earners spend their money locally, but Swami Satsangi and the team at the ashram were able, gradually, to get the construction and other needs supplied locally. They no longer needed to go to Deoghar or beyond for all their necessities.

With the young men of the community disproportionately engaged in the expanding number of activities being generated by the Swamis, ideas on how to engage the old and the very young members of the communities, together with the women, began to emerge. Many other novel opportunities began to rejuvenate a population previously, almost without exception, neglected and left to fend for themselves. A particularly innovative idea was to call the older widowed women to come to the ashram to engage in chanting. From eight in the morning until four in the afternoon, they would happily sing the Lord's name, *mala* beads in hand, 'Hare Rama Hare Rama Rama Rama Hare Hare: Hare Krishna Hare Krishna Krishna Krishna Hare Hare.' In this way, they got themselves out of their homes where they would normally be bound all day, present themselves at the ashram, perform their 'heavenly jobs' and finally, be paid at the end of the day, on a comparable basis with their younger counterparts. Physically improved by the act of mobilising themselves, psychically invigorated through the positive vibrations of mantra chanting and the energetic environment, but most importantly, they were proud that they could also contribute to providing for their families' needs. Altogether, it was an enriching experience for themselves and for those they interacted with on a daily basis. As Swami Satyananda explained:

> The physical ecosystem depends on the spiritual ecosystem. If the spiritual ecosystem of a place gets spoilt then the physical ecosystem cannot improve either.

Thus the elders were taking care of the spiritual ecosystem pervading the atmosphere, ensuring the right vibrations to enable the younger members of the community to effectively take care of the physical ecosystem. And, of course, these positive vibrations were carried on into the homes, altogether creating a far more nurturing environment for the many developing families.

Many other programmes and plans were initiated. Another example was support to those who wanted to open shops to address the growing needs of the enriched community. Now, on 8 September of every year, the birth anniversary of Swami Sivananda, this opportunity is bestowed on a selected villager, helping the local base of entrepreneurs to grow continuously. To ensure the sustainability of these outlets, help and guidance is given for the running and maintenance of the shops. Lakshman Mody was one of the many fortunate to be given the opportunity to open his own shop, but since he was physically challenged, bringing a regular supply of goods to sell from his premises was not a simple matter. But just as there was a solution for the many problems that continuously arose, a resolution for this particular issue soon transpired. Unexpectedly, a tricycle was donated to the ashram among the mounting supply of resources that were arriving on a regular basis. It was all that was needed to make Mr. Mody's simple life so much easier, this basic mode of transport enabling him and his daughters to make a sufficient living for their daily needs.

So life in the *panchayat* or village of Rikhia continued to develop, benefiting the people, a new vibrancy evident. Swami Satsangi was openly declared by her guru as the founder of the Rikhia ashram in every way. She had arrived in Rikhia unaware of Indian rural life, coming from an era that Swami Satyananda described as:

> A generation in India where girls today prefer to 'snack and dance'. Put on a Michael Jackson CD... [Swami Satsangi was] so ignorant of rural life that she did not even know the difference between a cow and a bull.

But her previous lack of experience in rural matters was certainly not a hindrance to her. As we could have anticipated, Swami Satsangi had readily gained a deep insight and understanding of the lives and needs of her neighbours. To all around her she was clearly a leading light, steadfast in facing the numerous challenges that inevitably arose in such an undertaking. Swami Satsangi was fully in control of the affairs around her, just as she had taken charge of all that she had encountered in her life thus far; a strong, formidable woman focused on the multitude of tasks at hand as the ashram activities expanded to support the ever more sophisticated developments of their rural community. Swami Satsangi worked day and night to ensure the smooth implementation of every vision for betterment. She contributed physically as she energetically involved herself in action, whether in construction, kitchen or other duties. She contributed also by emotionally motivating those around her to manage their personal challenges – she was involved in the regular *kirtans* ensuring rejuvenation for all involved in the relentless chores and she listened patiently to her neighbours' requests for needs to be fulfilled. She even contributed financially, using the funds she had surrendered from her long-forgotten past life to kick-start the Rikhia developments. But most importantly, she ensured that her beloved guru could continue with his *sadhana* unhindered by these relatively mundane matters.

When I discussed those early days in the development of Rikhia with the few people who were there at that time, they were all universal in their admiration for Swami Satsangi. They were amazed by her involvement in every activity, how she participated even in the process of building with such energy. She could be seen amidst the builders on the roof, advising men on constructing the rooftops, following up on others digging drains, in the grounds ensuring trees were being planted correctly and in the appropriate spots, in the kitchen giving instructions. She seemed to be everywhere, giving advice, shouting orders and, generally, in full control of all that was developing around her. And she also gave others the confidence to do the same. A young Swami from those days recounted how she had been sent to inspect a delivery of sand with no clue about what she should be looking for. Remembering how Swami Satsangi handled such situations, she worked out a way to determine its quality and gained the immediate respect of the men when she refused to accept the first delivery. She is still in the ashram, a leading light in the community with a deep understanding of all that needs to be done to keep the ashram running on a daily basis and in accordance with the strictly adhered to timetable of events.

That those around Swami Satsangi were greatly impressed by her energy is not surprising. But Swami Satsangi herself was equally astounded at how she was able to sustain the level of effort required to manage her way through each and every day. It was clear to her that she was functioning on a somewhat 'extraordinary' level. Not in her wildest dreams would she have envisaged that she would have the command of the delivery of such a vast array of tasks, that she would play so many diverse roles – mother, sister, guide, mason, plumber, gardener – nothing was unknown to her and neither was there anything too big or too insignificant for her attention when requested to undertake a job to be done.

Catalyst for Change

Swami Satsangi and the others supporting the developments in Rikhia were eager witnesses to the positive change in mood in their local community. The vibrant energy that pervaded the atmosphere was encouragement enough for their efforts to gain momentum and enable them to continuously adapt to face newly emerging challenges. The Swamis' efforts had been focusing on providing support to achieve a sustainable approach to meeting the villagers' basic requirements of food and shelter. In so doing they saw some pride and dignity instilled in the minds of all as working fathers could take care of their own families and mothers could provide a more substantial meal to their families at the end of a typically long, arduous day of chores.

While abject poverty was evidently diminishing and the lifestyle improving, the large population of children, however, were still languishing at home, carrying out the daily round of menial household duties, farming chores and tending to younger siblings. Few of the youth had access to, or even the remotest desire for any formal education. The few schools that did exist in this vicinity at that time were largely unattended, poorly equipped and barely maintained. No official bodies were interested either in enforcing the supposed compulsory attendance; no one had the energy or saw the point in making any change in the status quo. No one at all really gave any thought to the plight of these youngsters – the adult population, uneducated themselves, were unable to see any benefits that could arise from their offspring attending school; their children's futures were already destined to remain as theirs and their forefathers had been before them. The future they focused on was to make just enough to survive the daily trials and tribulations of their lives.

A radical change would have to occur in the lives of these people if they were ever to be shaken out of their torpid existence. And, as experience widely informs us, ultimately education is considered as the only possible solution that could bring about a long-term and a much needed sustainably improved future for a thriving community.

The catalyst for a fundamental change in direction for the neglected youth was initiated one day from a quite unexpected source. A young girl from the nearby village of Nawadih visited the ashram. Quite puzzled by the unexpected visitor, Swami Satsangi spoke directly with her, asking her why she had come. She simply stated: 'Swamiji, I want to learn English.'

These few words so innocently spoken, on later reflection quite profound, came as a complete surprise. Here was a young girl in tatters, no doubt often suffering due to a lack of proper nutrition and clean water, almost devoid of any formal education – and all she wanted to do was to learn English, having, like many others, been in awe as she had witnessed Swami Satsangi's command of everything around her, something they had never seen a woman do before.

Initially, Swami Satsangi could not see the benefit in such a request. What earthly good would a few words of English do for an impoverished child in this rural community? Surely, teaching English could not be the best use of a Swami's precious time. But after due consideration and discussion within the small group, the Swamis decided that they should consider their young neighbour's unexpected desire. And so it was that with this one simple request, the platform was set for a sea-change in this unsuspecting community.

As is so often the case, it is the simple way that children perceive life in their uninhibited and innocent way that enables them to be the precursors of change in our societies. It was this quality that made the ashram-dwellers think of English lessons, all because of this single student, the young girl who had mustered up the courage to knock at Swami Satsangi's door and openly declare her wish. One student soon became several, though attendance was initially sporadic. Over time, many more subjects were added to the list of young aspiring students, starting with English; later, teaching of computer skills were added. Soon the young visitors also took an interest in yoga and other activities that they witnessed during their regular visits. As the mental capacity of the young girls sharpened, they started to observe ashram life and the behaviour of their Swami teachers. Quite deliberately, their teachers never brought any attention to the unkempt, dirty appearance of their young charges. Unintentionally, however, the girls were being subtly influenced by their new mentors that they identified with as role models worthy of emulation. Then steadily, without any instruction, the girls started to take more care of their physical appearance also.

In the Rikhia of today, not one of Swami Satsangi's neighbours goes to sleep hungry at night. Every child receives five or six new outfits in a year, no longer second-hand donations but specifically ordered to sizes that fit each individual. The schools are now full, with classrooms that have been upgraded to make an inviting environment for studies. Lessons are taught by staff who have an interest in their students' results and study is a passion for many youngsters who are now burning with ambitions to lead a life quite different from their earlier assumed inevitably dull, stark destinies. Two private schools have even opened in the vicinity as the parents' demands for quality has risen. And, whereas in the past the students had to walk long distances in their bare feet to get themselves to school, whether in summer or winter, now many are to be seen proudly making their way on their new bicycles donated by the ashram.

Lessons in English and computer studies continue to be taught in the ashram, along with yoga, dance, music, arts and crafts. The lessons extend to the *batuk*s, the young boys in the community – their total numbers now reach around 1600 students. With only a few swamis available to cater to all the demands, older children also assist in the teaching of younger novices, thus developing a self-sustaining system which brings confidence to all.

Swami Satsangi herself has been quite astonished by the remarkable change in this population – quite clearly, the place that she had entered in September 1989 could not be recognised as the same place today. In a *satsang* given in Rikhia in 2007 Swami Satsangi recounted:

> When I arrived with Swami Satyananda at Rikhia, an obscure village in Jharkhand, I felt as if I was slipping back into the sixteenth century. You could not get more backward than that; there was no trace of the twenty-first century, no roads, no electricity, no phones, no newspapers, no cars, no busy streets, no hospitals, a few dilapidated schools looking desolate with a few ragged unkempt children, wearing torn and tattered clothing....
>
> Today, when you see the same place and the people, especially the children, you may not believe the condition they were in hardly ten years before. They would qualify perfectly for a before and after advertisement....
>
> The very same children, who at that time did not have the confidence to even look anyone in the eye and answer a simple question like '*aapka naam kya hai?,* what is your name?', today are at the helm of the Rikhia ashram, speaking wonderful English, designing the ashram calendars, conducting all

its multifarious programmes, singing soul-stirring *kirtan*s, conducting *yajna*s [ritual offerings] with perfect intonation of Sanskrit mantras which would make even a pandit [Vedic master] sit up and listen.

When I look back to the time where a young village girl knocked on our door and shyly asked to learn English and we hesitantly started to teach her 'abc', I am amazed to see how the small seed sown on that day has flourished into this giant tree of over 1,500 children that are ever on the increase.

The small village of Pania Pagaar in Rikhia, where the ashram stands, is a fitting place for such a turnaround in the events of its inhabitants' lives. The meaning of the village's name is 'plentiful water', which is metaphorically and physically apt. Just as any trees, flowers, fruits or shrubs planted by the new residents have remarkably flourished with a continuous supply of crystal-clear water from the well, so too, people grew and blossomed. Not a single person has been left out of these developments – the entire area was considered the ashram, it was not limited only to the area defined by boundary walls and occupied by Swami Satsangi and the devotees of Swami Satyananda. Like a family, each person felt the pain of others and remedies were jointly sought and implemented.

The philosophy is very simple. The entire panchayat [village] is my ashram. Every house is my house. Their pains and pleasures are my own. Their poverty is my poverty and their happiness is my happiness. If anyone is sick it is my ashram inmate who is sick. This is not a social philosophy, it is Vedantic philosophy. You have to see yourself in everyone and you have to see everyone within your own self.

Swami Satyananda, 2002, p. 187

Swami Satyananda spoke often in his *satsangs* about the changes brought about in Rikhia, how, with some initial support and guidance, the circumstances of a group of people could be so readily improved in a sustainable way. He urged others to do as they had done, a few unselfish acts for the betterment of all, indeed the many BSY-affiliated centres around the world perpetually play a role in bringing about improvements of others in their local communities whether similarly supporting rural, developing areas such as Rikhia, or working with the rehabilitation of prisoners in London or other major cities of the world. Not just the receivers benefiting from these unselfish acts, the givers also deriving pleasure from the flourishing happiness around them. Importantly though, Swami Satyananda was well aware of the stark fact that no one is immune to the detrimental effect that one's impoverished neighbours can potentially have on one's own circumstances, a situation of 'haves' and 'have nots' is absolutely not a long-term option in one locale. The vicious cycle of life this rural community had accepted as their natural lot was broken and transformed; he foresaw that as the young people in this community had been benefited, so they in turn would work for the welfare of other rural communities. Just as prosperity was slowly but steadily growing in Rikhia, others would begin to do likewise.

On the physical plane, the results of Swami Satsangi's far-reaching efforts under the guidance of her guru in Rikhia are evident for anyone to see. For the young girls of school-going age, for example, English, computer skills, yoga, dance, music and other activities have been taught directly in the ashram for several years. They have also been given bicycles to assist them in getting to school, and significantly improved attendance records and exam results are being attained. The next generation of young newlywed women too often receive small wedding gifts to provide a small start in the formation of their new lives and, by now, some of the attendees of the ashram activities are children of children who were the pioneers of these early beginnings.

Working women, too, are assured of their rights, able to take advantage of exemplary working conditions and entitled to equal pay to their male co-workers. They were also freed from the unnecessary burden of wearing absurdly unsuitable clothing for the roles they have to play – the sari, the generally accepted compulsory dress of a married woman, could be replaced with more practical jeans during working hours.

Widows in the Rikhia area are no longer family outcasts, forced by their late husbands' families to lead a life of misery. Now they are regarded with respect in a society known for its past mistreatment of people such as these who have been made to endure hardship and deprivation. Older women of the community are looked after during their retirement years to enable them to continue to live in dignity in this society, rather than being viewed as unwanted millstones around the necks of their already overburdened families.

And so it is that women in Rikhia have the relative 'luxury' of living in secure conditions, with the peace of mind that comes from knowing that whatever befalls them at any age, Swami Satsangi and the ashram are there to ensure that their lives are free of unnecessary stress and anxiety. Such security in life is something that all humans naturally seek but seldom find, a state of mind denied, or not taken up, by the vast majority of society, but a state of mind that now evidently pervades the minds of these women, women who for centuries were amongst the most neglected in society. As Swami Satyananda once said, 'In India women have been exploited, ill-treated, dishonoured and weakened...' He considered such treatment of women as a crime against basic humanity, particularly sickening given that women, as he rightly asserted, are 'the epitome of God's grace and beauty'.

But it is not these actions alone that can change the plight of women; it is not enough just to deal with worldly support mechanisms to enable women to live in peace that will see a change in the gender balance involved in world affairs, spiritual or otherwise. Nor is it enough for women to be busy with cottage industry activities, sitting at home or in a village green or hall making small household items, arts and crafts and so on. Small ventures such as these are commonly springing up in ever-increasing numbers around developing societies and supported mainly by the well-wishers of society. The NGOs, for instance, certainly make a difference in everyday lives, but these ventures are not life-changing, not truly transforming the heart of society. Swami Satyananda and Swami Satsangi both knew this – they understood that a certain level of aggression from women was required to truly make a difference.

But where to start? Women of society cannot hold only men to account for the current state of world affairs; the fact that neither political landscapes, boardroom demographics nor spiritual hierarchies have a healthy number of female representatives is not entirely due to the bullishness of men barring the way to women members. There is a degree of self-abuse that has to be considered, a self-limiting nagging voice that often prevents developments happening in the lives of women as they rightly should. In the words of the Irish writer Sue Leonard:

> There's so much talk about glass ceilings and men as obstacles
> to women, and that wasn't my experience when I worked in
> a man's world. But women are set up to think of themselves
> as being agents of guilt. They do it to each other and society
> does it to them. You can't pick up a magazine without being
> told how to live.

Intellectually, women know absolutely that they are fit for 'higher things'; even men can intellectualise on these matters and not fail to draw the same conclusions. And we see that this is so as the vast majority of our male-led corporations, year after year, diligently set diversity targets to demonstrate that they are willing for change. But they do this comfortable in the knowledge that, with no personal consequence to these same men, the balance is hardly shifting at all. This perpetuated situation of male dominance is not a feature of only developing countries, there is a large deficit in women leaders in the developed nations of the world also. Clearly, legislation, targets or any number of other actions half-heartedly set in motion will not have the necessary impact that will ultimately lead to global change.

Swami Satyananda stated:

> The message for the awakening of woman will go out from [Rikhia, Deoghar].

Swami Satyananda, 2007, p. 37

I firmly believe that the foresightedness of Swami Satyananda will, as typically it does, become manifest now in this regard; the awakening to the truth of women's worth will indeed go out from Rikhia. Swami Satyananda took a quite different approach to bring about a change in women's place in today's society in the obvious recognition of the fact that world events were not going nearly far enough in bringing about some semblance of balance in societal affairs. Swami Satyananda, in his ultimate wisdom, had begun to tackle the apparent gender disparity in his own way in this community where he had been well established as its leader. He recognised that the psyche of young girls, not grown women already conditioned by societal norms and unable to come out of their patterned ways of behaviour, had to be changed. The place to start had to be with the young impressionable *kanya*s of Rikhia, young girls in their developmental years, the impressionable, healthy minds of youth. As is common in parts of India at certain times in the year, Swami Satyananda too put these *kanyas* on a pedestal and following age-old Vedantic practices showered them with love and blessings and, in so doing, he imparted a self-worth, a self-belief in these young minds, a belief not at an intellectual level but rather, with a heartfelt knowledge of women's true place in the world order. And now these young girls, many now young women, truly know their own worth, their greatness also ingrained deep within their psyche. Anyone who has had the opportunity to meet them can readily testify this to be so. These young women have such a confidence in themselves, but also that innocence and purity of young mind is also still very much in evidence. Swami Satyananda's sheer brilliance, his true grasp of the real plight of women and the actions he was compelled to take with Swami Satsangi, an accomplished and confident role model, leading the way, had begun to bring his vision to life.

As that first group of youngsters who commenced their English classes some years back are now nearing the end of their formal educational years, we are already seeing this vision come to fruition. A small start is reflected in the life of a young woman who started her involvement with the ashram when she was just three years old. She now commutes to her work in a bank, is an active participant in ashram activities just as she has always been; her emerging career a reality that could not have been dreamed of for the generations that went before her.

Rikhia of Today

The day of Swami Satsangi's arrival in 1989 at this small village of Rikhia, as is well established, was a defining moment that prompted a profound and permanent change in the lives of people residing in this vicinity. On arrival in Rikhia some twenty years ago, the sole intention of this initially small group of stalwart disciples, was to be close to their guru and support him in his personal *sadhana*. But when Swami Satyananda received the divine message to help his neighbours, there was a collective compulsion for this close-knit team to work ever more determinedly towards changing the circumstances of the community of downtrodden people that had barely scraped by on the meagre resources available to them. They knew that such a disparity of situations between those inside the ashram – even though the Swamis' lifestyle was certainly not luxurious but had a certain surety in their circumstances – and those outside could not coexist in harmony forever. They knew also what an immense task lay ahead to address such anomalies, a task once initiated that could not subsequently be given up lightly. Resolutely, they joined forces to embark on a structured, disciplined process of change commensurate with the need of the moment, a journey that, without doubt in anyone's mind, would be undeniably daunting. It should also be recognised, however, that this was not a one-way exchange, one group giving and the other receiving but rather, this was a mutual cohabitation of two quite disparate groups, a symbiotic relationship in effect. The skills of the local community was essentially needed, in turn, to assist in the provision of basic necessities that were effectively supporting this small band of Swami infiltrators. With these two groups, the Santalis and the *Sannyasins* in Rikhia, comfortable in each other's presence, effectively leaning on one another through the trials, tribulations and joys of life, a relative calm pervaded the surrounding atmosphere. The daily rituals could have quite happily continued in this vein, with boundaries loosely defined but well understood, a status quo comfortably enjoyed from day to day, month to month.

However, no matter how well Narayana's secure boundary walls had been constructed to build a barrier around Swami Satyananda, no matter that the guru had left Munger with no intention to establish anything concrete, his only goal to continue his personal *sadhana*, his quest to know the absolute truth of life, it was quite evident that while Swami Satyananda still existed on this earth, his devotees would always seek to be in his presence.

As Swami Satyananda heeded the call to take action in his

local neighbourhood, the news of his temporary emergence from solitude was quickly and unavoidably in the public domain. Succumbing to pressure, he allowed people to visit Rikhia for a fleeting visit.

The Munger ashram had hosted the international yoga convention in October 1993 and, as this event was coming to a close, people were invited to visit the Rikhia ashram on the following day to hear a *satsang* by Swami Satyananda. The day, 1 November 1993, saw the first opportunity for 'outsiders' to step inside the Rikhia boundary walls and observe for themselves what was beginning to unfold in this unique environment. Although the opportunity to enter Rikhia was given at what could only be considered short notice, thousands flocked to see this new place and, more importantly, to receive the *darshan* of their reclusive guru. Those wishing to avail of this unexpected opportunity were asked to visit the Shiva temple in Deoghar before entering Rikhia, a mandate they happily followed. Devotees were then allowed to enter this enigmatic place, but departing with the stark message ringing in their ears that this was not (yet) a sign that Rikhia was open for visitors rather, the opposite was true.

This as we know now, of course, is history – Rikhia today is a thriving hive of activity. On entering the ashram grounds, one is struck by the sight of such a high-quality establishment in this most rural of locations. The infrastructure is always in pristine condition, the gardens beautifully landscaped, with an abundant variety of plants and trees. The Rikhia Ashram is such an immensely pleasant venue for an ambitious series of annual

programmes – events like Shivaratri Yoga Sadhana, Chaitra
Navaratri Sadhana, Akshay Tritiya, Sri Vidya Puja, Guru
Purnima, Saundarya Lahari Retreat, Sat Chandi Mahayajna and
many more. Several intensive courses such as Kriya Yoga and
tattwa shuddhi, yogic studies, teachers' training, yoga sadhana
and ashram life, *prana vidya* and others, all undertaken here
by eminent speakers and teachers. And many of these events,
quite unique in their content, founded on books such as *Sri
Saundarya Lahari, Sri Vijana Bhairava, Tattwa Shuddi* and
others that somehow, through all else that she was able to
achieve, Swami Satsangi also managed to author – detailed and
scholarly works on yogic philosophy never in the past brought
together to such a high standard.

Many of these programmes are completed within a few
days, and others last for periods of up to four months, some
now for duration of a full year; some are designed for a
handful of people, others catering to thousands of participants
converging to attend. While these many programmes are in
progress, side by side, the work in supporting and working
with the local community continues. The queues for the regular
clinics continue, the local people have a strong belief that the
treatment they receive there is somehow superior to what they
may receive elsewhere and, additionally, the poorest to the poor
are treated with utmost respect. With tuberculosis no longer
a concern, some effort has been made in helping people to
regain their eyesight. In 2013, for example, many doctors from
across the world visited the ashram to assist in the treatment
of people with cataracts; together with the support of local

hospitals, more than a hundred people were effectively treated and their sight restored.

All events, big or small, are run to exact timing and direction, but lovingly and sensitively, orchestrated by the dedicated Swamis who reside in Rikhiapeeth to fulfil the many tasks required of them. Their tasks involve assigning accommodation, ensuring clean bedding, providing plentiful and delicious *satwik* food, the pure unadulterated, nutritious, vegetarian meals that are a welcome feature for all, to event management and coordination of the calendar of activities. All these roles are undertaken with undeniable acts of selfless service. The *sannyasins* here are not interested in achieving worldly recognition for all that they are called on to do – their aims lie in quite different directions. The residents of Rikhia quite 'simply' want to know themselves, to know their very core, the innermost depths of their souls, and it is to this objective that their whole lives are dedicated, this and this alone. And alongside the *sannyasins,* the young of the local community can be seen in the forefront of all the activities, amazing everyone present with displays of traditional and modern dancing alike, seeing that everyone is properly seated and attended to, their unwavering voices leading the many complex chanting programmes – in reality, many of the ashram's activities are being designed and led by those that were, in the very recent past, quite literally, the rejects of society.

And though these events necessarily run with military-like precision, the essence of what makes Rikhia unique is prevalent. Right from the mantras, the cornerstone words that are chanted in the ashram, the mantras *Aim, Hreem, Klim,* the seed sounds, the mantra of creation, the mantra of energy and prosperity and the mantra of fulfilment and transformation, these sounds together invoke divine vibrations that are instrumental in helping us to curb negative energies. Then the *Sri Yantra,* the symbol that depicts the ever-present spirit of Devi and the welcoming 'Namo Narayan' greeting that is heard reverberating all around, show that Rikhia is a place of unconditional, divine love, peace and understanding. They indicate the softer, gentler, feminine aspects of divinity often lacking in other such establishments. And although large crowds of people attend these events, the pervading atmosphere remains one of calm serenity, an ambience often remarked upon by the thousands who visit from all corners of the globe. Rikhia today has not lost its tranquillity either – the buffaloes, the birds and the insects, trees, plants, crickets, frogs, music, children's laughter and the breeze in the air are all still very much in evidence. Nothing of the beauty of this rural place has been lost, only added to.

People go there for one of the many events or just to be near their guru in the rejuvenating confines that have become synonymous with Swami Satsangi's world-renowned Rikhiapeeth. Love reverberates in the ashram air, and it is this that makes Rikhia unique.

> *'Love is the energizing elixir of the universe, the cause and effect of all harmonies...'*

Maulana Jalaluddin Rumi

Thus the birth – the awakening – of the Rikhia ashram had begun. The underlying principles and objectives that underpinned the ashram's objectives were consistent with those first espoused by Adi Shankaracharya and enshrined in the Sivananda and now the Satyananda ashrams. The underlying substance of Rikhia, however, became somewhat different. Rikhiapeeth is not so much a place where one would go to 'to do' – rather Rikhia, from the outset, was intended as a place emphatically just 'to be'. Many people who visit these ashrams refer to Munger as the *head and hands* of Satyananda yoga, while Rikhia is referred to as the *heart*, the difference in atmosphere quite palpably felt by all. The Munger ashram was founded under the auspices of Swami Satyananda's *sankalpa,* his resolve handed down to him by his guru, to 'take yoga from shore to shore and door to door'. This duty was fulfilled by the time he left Munger, the culmination of twenty years of dedication to this task and a place that is very much alive today under the guidance of Swami Niranjan. Rikhia, on the other hand, was founded on the *sankalpa* Swami Satyananda fully focused his attention on in his final years, his undertaking more resolutely to 'serve, love and give' – also in accordance with his guru's guidance. With Swami Satsangi, unwavering in her resolve to serve her guru, constantly by his side, the perfect combination was in place to enact this resolve. The vision that had transpired from the consciousness of Swami Satyananda and the energy of Swami Satsangi combined together to achieve their common goal and the truly deserving, needy population, after centuries of neglect, could embrace a new way of living through a mutual atmosphere of love and trust for the benefit of all. Rikhia saw the beginning of a new era for Swami Satyananda, Swami Satsangi and the other Swamis who had gone there in the selfless pursuit of serving others. This was to be the era of Bhakti, the era of divine love where all activities were directed towards 'a higher purpose' as enshrined in the nine volumes of *Bhakti Yoga Sagar*, a beautiful treatise consisting of just a few of the numerous and insightful *satsangs* given by Swami Satyananda during this period of his life.

Behind Rikhia stands a story of enormous success and change. It is no longer the Rikhia that was 'discovered' in 1989, a period that now seems like a distant past for the local community. And this has been achieved through the steady commitment, dedication and devotion of Swami Satsangi.

As in any establishment, there are certain house rules, a certain recognisable, but sometimes not clearly definable, decorum to follow. All ashrams also have their own way of being, their culture and identity that even a visitor adopts while within their confines. Satyananda ashrams around the world, whether in Australia, Colombo, Greece or India, do not belong to any individual soul; they do not belong to anyone at all in particular. In keeping with the meaning of the word 'ashram' derived from the Sanskrit *shram*, to labour, residents and visitors alike are expected to undertake periods of *seva*, selfless service, such as cleaning and chopping vegetables, serving food to the many visitors, or the much loved service of giving *prasad*, blessed gifts, to the countless local villagers coming together on many occasions throughout the year.

But first and foremost, the attitude that the scores of 'ashramers' need to imbibe during their stay at Rikhia is one of simply *being* and *feeling;* the events that take place there are *esoteric* in nature, stirring the very soul in an atmosphere that is 'different', the energy bewildering but nurturing in ways that our ordinary minds cannot readily understand. When you enter this ashram you must leave your intellect behind, listen to your heart and realise the change that happens deep down within you.

> Like the musk deer, we have everything in us. So it is that inner being which is being stirred by these mantras and rituals. They influence the etheric personality, not the subconscious mind and not the unconscious mind. We have read about conscious, subconscious and unconscious. Dr Sigmund Freud and others have explained it, but that is just the tip of the iceberg – man extends far beyond the unconscious.

Swami Satyananda, 2001, p. 94

Rikhia, we can say today, has an identity; the ashram there is a key and integral element of the Bihar School of Yoga, but yet a unique and special limb of this most revered fraternity of ever-growing institutions with the sole aim of bringing about an improvement in the life of man. Rikhia most certainly did not have an identity before, not in any positive sense at least, and the thread that runs through its growth and development is the unbounded energy of Swami Satsangi.

Swami's Beginning

This short book started off in my mind as a biography of Swami Satsangi, intended as a small, token gesture that would provide some limited insight into her life. However, as I struggled to capture the magnitude of what I wanted to portray about her into just a few pages, I came to a realisation that it was quite impossible to separate Swami Satsangi from her beloved guru.

This was a relationship that, I came to understand, had not just begun when Swami Satsangi gave up the career she had built in the corporate world to dedicate herself to an entirely different way of living, a life in search of spiritual enlightenment, a life without a trace of a personal ego, any ego long lost in the pursuit of selflessly supporting her guru and in the upliftment of others.

When I first started to discuss the compiling of this book with Swami Satsangi, I was, frankly, quite nervous and apprehensive, to say the least. Unexpectedly, I was driven to know more about this woman who had, despite all odds, risen to the top of her spiritual world, handling her burdens with ease. I struggled somewhat when we met, uncertain about how I should address her or act in front of her. Swami Satsangi, I first thought, was similar in stature to a Christian priest or a bishop and I had been conditioned in my own early years to revere such people only from afar, speaking only in the unlikely event of first being spoken to. Consequently, in the presence of this clearly established great leader, her pervading aura, her ability to effortlessly command attention, rendered my mind quite blank, any questions carefully considered and prepared for discussion suddenly seeming inconsequential and, therefore, often went unspoken. Thankfully, however, people with perceptive minds like Swami Satyasangananda's have an understanding of what a person needs to know and often, in subtle ways, broach the topic themselves.

In one of our early meetings, Swami Satsangi was reviewing something I had written about her as I sat quietly looking on, wondering what her response may be. I had referred to her as 'a saint' and as I sat somewhat tensely, unable to read any expression on her face to gauge her reaction, the only remark she made was, 'I'm not a saint.' This reminded me of a time I had gone to listen to her talk on the theme of 'Yoga for the Twenty-first Century' at the Satyananda ashram in Bangalore. During the event, a few youngsters were called forward to receive recognition for their achievements. One of the young boys presented to Swami Satyasangananda thanked her, calling her 'Ma'am' as is the standard practice across India when greeting a woman whom you respect but don't particularly know. 'I'm not "Ma'am"' came the resounding response, 'I'm Swami Satsangi.'

The way this young boy had approached Swami Satsangi without any inhibitions struck a chord with me. He had walked confidently towards centre-stage with absolutely no inhibitions and simply addressed the person before him in the way that he knew best. He also accepted the correction, thanked Swami Satsangi for his gift and went on his way. There was no trace of any discomfiture in his mind at all, the fleeting moment immediately forgotten. It was so refreshing to realise that if we as adults could become child-like from time to time, innocent and unconcerned about what others may think of us, life could be so much simpler. From that moment on, I resolved to drop any pretence or veneer of learning and merely be myself when I talked to Swami Satsangi. I knew that, as long as the right intentions were in my heart, I need not fear anything.

So after an initially shaky start, I sat reasonably comfortably in conversation with Swami Satsangi and asked her to talk about how the unusual life she was now leading had begun. She said:

> In India we have a tradition where our families have a relationship with a highly regarded person, someone who will be regularly called upon to give advice on a whole myriad of matters, not just spiritual. He is our 'guruji' [almost certainly a man] and we can ask him about what we need to do in matters related to business, how to do handle relationship issues, problems related to health, whether one should or

should not travel – quite literally, the guruji can be consulted on virtually anything under the sun. And, though we have this aspect of 'the family guru', it is not necessarily an exclusive relationship and so sometimes we would visit other gurus, people who may not be so close to us but whom we have a high regard for.

So one day when I was just twelve years old my parents took me to meet Swami Satyananda in Munger, which was quite a long way from our home in West Bengal, but my parents were keen to meet him – they had heard many good things about him.

I was very talkative then and as soon as I was introduced to this much sought-after guru, I quite boldly started asking him so many questions. I was most probably embarrassing my parents the way I was quite casually talking with him, but I somehow felt so comfortable in this great man's presence; I felt somehow that I knew him and I just carried on asking the questions that were effortlessly rising up in my mind. And many of my questions were quite strange to me – they were about topics that I had probably never even thought about before. But somehow they kept coming and I was happy to be receiving satisfactory answers, not at all concerned that I may be taking up more time than that allotted to be in his presence. Someone like Swami Satyananda would generally have a never-ending queue of people waiting to have their chance for a few moments of interaction.

During this first conversation, the young Satsangi quite boldly asked Swami Satyananda if he could give her *sannyas,* which meant she wanted him to allow her to be a Swami in the Satyananda ashram right there and then. She had no real idea then, of course, what it meant to take *sannyas,* but somehow the atmosphere in Munger, the *geru*-coloured clothes of the residents, the ashram, the energy – it all appeared so attractive that she felt she wanted to live there also.

Swami Satyananda did not dismiss Swami Satsangi offhand as most others may have done on hearing such a bold request from someone so young. Instead, he asked her if she understood what it meant to take *sannyas.* Without hesitation she replied, 'Yes… it means renunciation, *tyaag.'*

He asked her then, 'But what is it that you would renounce? I don't think you have anything. First you must get something, then you must talk about renunciation. Now, whatever you have, that is your father's, not yours… So become something, do something, get something. Then if you want to renounce, tell me.'

Swami Satsangi left Munger that day to carry on with her life as it had gone on before, this meeting with another 'new guru', just a fleeting encounter that readily receded to the back of her mind as she stepped outside the ashram boundary walls. Her life continued quite unperturbed by this brief interlude undertaken at the behest of her parents.

Several years later, however, and by then a young woman in her twenties, she saw a photograph of Swami Satyananda at a friend's home. She was almost mesmerised when she saw it. The face was familiar. She knew that she had met this person before but she could not immediately recollect who he was. The purpose of her visit to her friend's house was no longer foremost in her mind, she could only ask about the photo. Once Swami Satsangi realised that this was the Swami whom her parents had taken her to meet at the age of twelve, the memories of that first meeting came flooding back – how she had asked him so many questions that day and when satisfied with his responses, she had boldly asked him to give her *sannyas*. Inwardly smiling at the thought of her childhood innocence on that day, she lost no time in following up on what she had known all those years earlier was her rightful destiny. From this moment on, the minute she had caught sight of her guru's photograph, she knew that her life was set for a remarkable change. The photograph had an instant effect on her – a '*shakti path*' – and from that very moment she made all efforts to try to meet Swami Satyananda.

Swami Satsangi knew without doubt that she had found her true guru, the man who was to teach her all that was to become important in her life from then on. She occasionally wondered about the instant bond between them. She recalled the times that her parents would take her to Almora to visit her brothers who had gone there to study. While there, she would go horse-riding and speak with the guide as if she were speaking to a well-known friend; similarly, she used to have long conversations with the boatman at the lake, discussing topics that she could not have had any prior knowledge of. Her mother related these stories to her in later years, and told her she was puzzled at how she had acted then, speaking of matters beyond the comprehension of a child. It was later that she realised that Swami Satyananda originated from the area they had visited and she could only assume that there was some sort of past connection – there was simply no other explanation.

An immediate meeting could not be arranged. Swami Satyananda was travelling extensively at this time in his life and he was in South America then. Swami Satsangi was quite prepared to go to the length of travelling there to see him – she did not want to lose any more time away from this guru. It proved impossible, however, to arrange a meeting there and sometime later, at the earliest possible opportunity she set off to meet Swami Satyananda, once again in Munger.

As she walked through the gate of the ashram, for only the second time in her life, and just a few months after seeing the photograph that had triggered memories of their first meeting, she immediately felt that this place was to be her home. As they came face-to-face, Swami Satsangi had no hesitation whatsoever in asking him once again: 'Can I take *sannyas*?' Swami Satyananda responded with a clear 'Yes,' but told her his assent was subject to the fulfilment of certain conditions.

If Swami Satsangi was to enter ashram life, Swami Satyananda explained, this could only happen with her parents' explicit support for her to do so. He said to her: 'The first test that you have to take is to convince your parents and take their blessings. Because in *sannyas* life, you have to be independent, not dependent. You can renounce your finances, you can renounce your wealth, your status, but emotional independence – it is very difficult to renounce that because there's no use becoming dependent on a guru. You cannot even be dependent on me.'

For a young woman in India to extract her parents' blessings to become a *sannyasin* is no easy task. Although Swami Satsangi's parents had been extremely liberal and supportive of their daughter's chosen path so far, taking *sannyas*, becoming a dedicated disciple of one's chosen guru, was a step in a wholly different direction. It is not at all a problem to respect someone else's son or daughter cutting off family ties in this manner, but as we know in all matters, we only really appreciate the enormity of something when it happens to us. Until we are in a particular situation, we have no idea how we will react – we think we know, but in reality we don't. When something touches us deep down, when we have the experience, only then will we know how it feels to us.

A few years after entering ashram life, Swami Satsangi herself wrote a book on the guru–disciple relationship, what becoming a committed *sannyasin* (or disciple) entailed. In it she explained:

> Disciple is derived from the word 'discipline'. A disciple, therefore, is one who undergoes discipline in order to develop spiritually. In Sanskrit, a disciple is called *shishya* or 'one who is willing to learn'. Anyone who offers himself to [a] guru in order to discipline himself is a disciple. It does not matter if you relate his teachings to your spiritual welfare or material life. If you are receptive to his wisdom and follow his guidance, then you are a disciple.

Swami Satsangi, 2011, p. 42

As in any process of learning, there are varying 'degrees' of disciples or *sannyasins*, just as there are primary, secondary and tertiary levels of our standard methods of education. According to the 'Saraswati lineage' of *sannyasins* to which the Bihar School of Yoga is aligned, we can generally refer to two main classes of *sannyasins*: '*karma sannyasins*' and '*sadhaka sannyasins*'. Though somewhat an over-simplification, these two groups can be described thus: *karma sannyasins* may receive initiation from a guru in certain practices – they may choose to live with their guru for some time, a number of years even, but they do not totally 'surrender' themselves to the guru or renounce all their possessions, committed to living a life of service. They will hold their guru in high regard and consult him in personal and spiritual matters. Most often a *karma sannyasin* will live a 'normal life' outside the ashram, perhaps married with children, and carrying on a profession. People in this category may make regular visits to the guru to receive his blessings and guidance. In turn, they usually provide the guru with financial assistance or other support for the day-to-day running of the ashram and for the countless community programmes that the ashram would undertake – the Bihar School of Yoga, as we know, is a strong proponent of supporting social development programmes, in fact, this is the key reason for the very existence of Rikhia as it stands today. *Sadhaka sannyasins*, on the other hand, are those who come to realise that the material life in which they operate is no longer conducive to their spiritual development – they are internally compelled to change their way of life in search for a deeper meaning. It is not unusual that before entering into this life, the aspiring *sannyasin* would have already had some 'spiritual experiences' or 'inner awakenings'. Undoubtedly, for this type of person, a set of circumstances will transpire that lead him to his guru. When he has found his guru he will, when the guru determines he is ready, become a renunciate. Such a step is certainly not one that would be undertaken merely on a casual whim, the preparation undertaken before ultimate initiation would deter anyone who is not serious about taking this path.

> *Sannyas* is not a mere ritual of abandoning one's garments and donning the saffron robes, or shaving one's head and changing one's name. It has a deeper and greater significance than that. It is the process whereby one abandons one's ego, one's desires, one's selfish motivation, one's hypocrisies and shames and, above all, one's limited nature. It is for this that the *sannyasin* disciple strives.
>
> Swami Satsangi, 2011, p. 49

The Last Journey

You have gone on a journey in your youthful days
Of seeking and wondering who you are,
And what is the meaning and purpose of it all.
Journey on bravely, have no fear,
For now you are no longer alone.
You are protected by a mantle of love,

And unseen hands guide and direct you.

Though your footsteps may falter, your strength seem weak,

Be assured you will reach that goal that you seek.

Journey on bravely and if you feel tired,

Give yourself time to pause and reflect

On the glory of the sublime heights before you.

For if you get too fatigued, you may fall prey

To temptations of thoughts and return.

What have you left that demands your return?

Your days of worldly ambition are over,

Though you may not yet have fully grasped this fact.

You still feel you belong neither here not there,

But in truth you are already with me.

You have realised the emptiness of worldly life,

You have not attained to other planes of existence.

You are not certain of where you belong,

But I know who you are and where your home is,

And where you will find all the things that you seek.

What is past is over and cannot be restored.

It was all part of a journey of your soul,

And your search to find your real self.

You have begun to realise what you really are

And what the purpose of your life really is.

Swami Satsangi prior to her ashram days

The young initiate

Swami Satyananda and Swami Satsangi arriving in Colombo

Early days in Australia

Swami Satsangi joins the priests in worship in the Deoghar Temple

Getting by – Very basic facilities in the early days in Rikhia

Swami Satyasangananda gathering vital data from neighbours

Early days in construction of village homes

Priestly gatherings – Planting young trees in the ashram grounds

Paramhansa Satyananda during Panchagni Sadhana

Afterschool activities – Learning English at the ashram

Afterschool activities – Early days of computer studies

Young students visiting the ashram for yoga lessons

Visitors to the ashram packing *prasad* to be given to all

Patiently waiting to see the ashram doctor

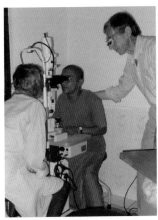

Doctor-swami and international contemporaries at the 2013 eye camp

Guru and Disciple, two bodies,

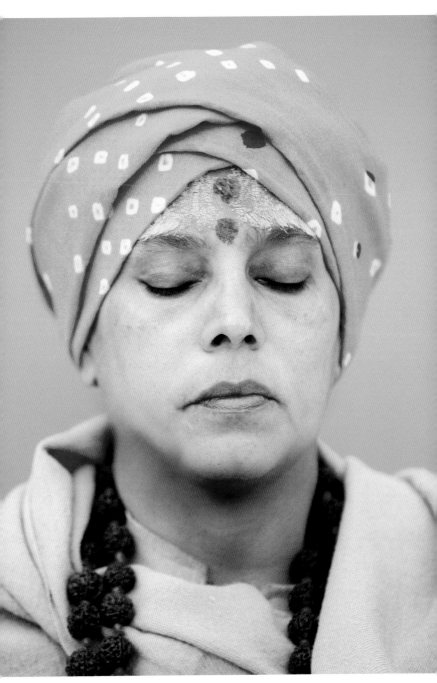

one intertwined living consciousness

Sat Chandi Yagna begins

Paramhansa Swami Satyananda looks on as the *kanyas* perform
traditional dances for international visitors during Sat Chandi Yagna

Swami Satsangi preparing to hand over a much
prized cow during *prasad* distribution

Paramhansa Swami Satyasangananda oversees *prasad*
distribution to the *kanyas* of Rikhia

Sat Chandi Yagna celebrations coming to a close

Paramhansa Swami Satyananda and his two 'flowers'

Two Beautiful Flowers
My wishes have all matured
And I have written the whole song.
Today my songs rise
From all directions of the world
And in the limelight
Of the moon and stars
Flows the light of your prana.
All the Vedas have been sung
And all the shastras *have been written.*
Today I have given the prana
Of my jnana *to all.*
And I have already given you everything
In the form of two beautiful flowers.

– Swami Satyananda

In days gone by, Guru and Disciple survey the ashram
grounds as they plan what's next

Swami Satyasangananda alone with her Guru after he passed to his next life

Yoginis of Tamil Nadu pay their respects to Swami Satyananda
during the sixth day funeral rite

Swami Satyasangananda at home in Rikhia

Swami Satyasangananda giving one of her many *satsangs*

Swami Satyasangananda returns to Melbourne as the guru

Paramhansa Swami Satyasangananda follows in
her Guru's footsteps in Panchagni Sadhana

If you return to the world now, you will be lost

And your life will have been spent in vain.

O child, keep your eyes fixed always on the goal!

You are my child who has returned to me.

Let me see who can keep you from me now.

You are surrounded by love and by light.

                              Swami Satyananda Saraswati

When she understood clearly what it meant to become a *sannyasin*, Swami Satsangi had to convince her parents to agree to her taking such a life-changing direction. Swami Satyananda went on to further explain to her what was required before she would be fully ready to proceed with such a commitment. He explained that in order to be a good *sannyasin*, to fulfil this role in any serious way, it was essential that she would become a 'strong and positive influence in the lives of others'. A *sannyasin* must be able to explain many aspects of life to people, about what they most likely would never have seen or may not even be able to comprehend on an intellectual basis. A *sannyasin* must have the capacity to inspire and convince others of the benefits of a different way of life, to be a solid rock to support someone should they falter along the way of this unknown path. Swami Satsangi knew herself well and the path that she was destined to follow. She knew that nothing but total commitment to the life of a *sannyasin* was the choice she had to make. She was also a sensitive, caring young woman – she loved the parents who had supported her in all that she had done in her life and she knew how deeply they loved and cherished her, their youngest child. So, although it was with unshakable conviction that Swami Satsangi confronted her parents to seek their blessings for her total surrender to her guru, she knew she had to renounce the life that she currently had. She had to live fully in the ashram, immersed in a life of service and duty, which effectively meant that her parents would, henceforth, lose their daughter, totally and forever. Never again would her parents feel their youngest child's fun-loving and energetic presence in the family home.

After preparing herself for the undoubtedly difficult conversation that she was to have, Swami Satsangi discussed three key points with her parents. She spoke about how *sannyasin*s were revered people, how throughout her life she had observed how her parents themselves would bow down in front of such people with a deep respect for the life of sacrifice that they followed, how they even idolised and supported their own guru's work. While her parents had not inculcated a strong ritualistic or spiritual element in their children's life, this reverence for a guru was etched in their minds. It was to this deep consciousness of reverence that she first appealed.

She then spoke of how she was evidently not destined to follow a career as a doctor, lawyer or engineer but neither was she entering into an undesirable life. Rather, the path that she wished to follow was an exalted life for someone with high ideals and goals who could make a real difference in the spiritual development of others' and a difference in society as a whole.

Finally, she discussed the benefits that they personally would reap from her chosen path. It is said that if someone follows the path of a *sannyasin*, when someone renounces all that they have for a path of spiritual development and the betterment of society, the family of the renunciate will also be blessed. They will receive the benefits of the *sannyasin*'s sacrifices, not just for the existing generation, but for the seven generations that have gone before and for the next seven generations yet to come.

Just as Swami Satsangi's parents had always supported their daughter's wishes and desires in the past, with somewhat heavy hearts, they once again gave her their blessings, blessings they gave with the hope that she would one day return to them. It was a hope to be unfulfilled, however, as we now know.

Swami Satsangi moved as naturally into this new life as she had done as a young woman leaving home for the first time to go to university in a new city and from the university to a career in another city:

> As I sat down with my parents to put my request to them, it was fully in the knowledge that to lose a child from your family was no small thing. We were a close family and I knew that this would not be an easy conversation to have. But though trembling as I had delivered my prepared words to my parents that day, I knew that I had no choice but to follow my chosen path and I remained steadfast throughout the discussion that had ensued. Of course I was elated when they gave me their blessings to continue on this path, but empathy for them did not immediately leave me.
>
> Physically, it was relatively easy for me to move on. I didn't have a complicated life at all that I had to extract

myself from here and there. I had quite a straightforward life, no complicated financial or relationship obligations, no unfulfilled commitments or worldly desires at all. So once I had been given the support of my family, it was quite straightforward for me to take the next step. It was a momentous time, of course, but it didn't seem so at the time – for me, it was the most natural transition, just moving on from one thing to something else. And then when I had moved, it was like a dark veil had been hanging over me, it was such a relief as I felt it suddenly and immediately drop. Soon I didn't remember anything of the past. I forgot everything completely... my work, my friends, my family, everything just disappeared as if from some distant past life.

Shakti Manifest

After several days of preparation for her initiation ceremony, days of purification of mind and body, periods of isolation and *mouna,* a deep and profound contemplative silence, followed by seemingly endless chanting of mantras and prayers, Swami Satsangi was ready to perform the solemnisation of her new life...

Aum Bhu Sannyastam Maya

I renounce everything in this earthly world

Aum Bhuvah Sannyastam Maya

I renounce everything in the astral plane

Aum Svaha Sannyastam Maya

I renounce everything in the heavenly plane

Aum Bhu Sannyastam Maya

I renounce everything in these three planes, earthly, astral and heavenly ...

At the Munger ashram, by the sacred Ganga, on 6 July 1982, just as the day was beginning to dawn, after these unambiguous words of total renunciation, she stepped out of the ritual waters. Donning her *geru* clothes and with shaven head, Swami Satyasangananda Saraswati, the disciple who would from then on imbibe the qualities of someone resolutely associated with knowing the truth and all else that the Saraswati lineage of *sannyasins* lived for was 'born'. Swami Satsangi, as we know her now, a young and brave woman, had totally surrendered her comfortable position in life, had given all her material possessions away and she had even broken her familial associations – all this in the knowledge, without any shadow of a doubt, that she was doing what she was meant to do. She knew that she was following her rightful destiny as she prepared to lay down her life to her guru and in service to others. She had arrived at these conclusions, however, not through an intellectual process of analysis, a decision pondered over at length and discussed with others. No, she knew only deep down in the furthest recesses of her heart that this was what she had been born to do.

Swami Satsangi recalled the moment of this momentous, life-changing, ceremonial occasion, 'With the ceremonies over, I felt like I had just been bathing in the wondrously pure and cool waters of the Ganga. I felt that a pure light had totally cleansed me from deep within, as if a spark of light had filled my core being with a wonderfully revitalised energy. I felt that I was catapulted into a totally different dimension of life and experience – quite literally, I felt as if I had just been born again in the same body.'

There was no time available to her now to bask in these wonderful moments. Her guru, Swami Satyananda Saraswati, firmly believed that all the Vedantic rituals were necessary to transform a life of ordinariness to a sublime one and he performed these complex rituals precisely to the letter, each and every step vested with its own significance. But once the ceremony was over, the new life of the *sannyasin* immediately began.

Swami Satyananda was a practical man who would never waste his precious time on superficial pleasantries. He, as his newly initiated disciple already understood, was a tough task master who demanded that his disciples were competent in all areas of ashram living. They had to be able to look after the buildings and grounds from basic cleaning to construction and gardening; administration and management tasks had to be understood down to the most basic detail, each considered as important as understanding the complex yogic sciences, since everything had its place in life. His temperament was a far cry from his own guru, Swami Sivananda, a man for whom he had the utmost reverence to the end of his life, but whose gentle way he felt no inclination to emulate. He explained what qualities his disciple should have:

> My disciple should have no superiority complex. [S]he is not a dry philosopher who spends all h[er] time and energy in preaching alone. [S]he has self-sacrifice and serves the world with h[er] silent and intense *sadhana*. In the midst of intense service, [s]he learns the way to rivet the mind on the *lakshya*,

the goal. [S]he is rooted in the idea: 'The world is a long dream, perishable. Truth alone is real.' For my student there is no world. [S]he perceives the divinity behind all names and forms.

My disciple has divine qualities. [S]he is noble gentle and soft. [S]he has abundant mercy, [s]he never begs. [S]he gives and gives and gives. [S]he has a large heart. [S]he mixes with all and loves everyone. [S]he sings the Lord's name. [S]he does *japa* and meditation. [S]he practises *asana* and *pranayama*. [S]he is very efficient in doing service. [S]he practises the yoga of synthesis. [S]he knows thought control.

[S]he is a practical *vedantin*. [S]he does cooking, proofreading, typing, nursing, lecturing, writing; [s]he can conduct classes, [s]he can disseminate spiritual knowledge, yet [s]he is simple and humble. [S]he serves the poor with love. [S]he has perfected tolerance for all faiths. [S]he talks little. [S]he is ever silent but dynamic. Work is worship for such a disciple. The spirit of service is ingrained in h[er]. [S]he is a Bhakta, a yogi and a *jnani*, all three combined in one.

Swami Satyananda

There were no concessions made to anyone who chose to take up this arduous, but utmost rewarding, life of austerities. Swami Satsangi had no option but to throw her whole self absolutely and completely into her new life. On the material plane, it was a meagre existence, with basic but nourishing meals at fixed times of the day, only two to three sets of simple clothing, no air-conditioning in the hot summers or a warming fire in the cold night air of northern winters – such luxuries had to be forgotten along with all other aspects of her relatively pampered previous existence. With a new and vital source of seemingly endless energy kindled by this new awakening, there was no time available to give any thought to such material comforts. In any case, there was not a single second available for recounting the past gone by and certainly no longing on her part to think of her old life. Her past was cast off just as one would let go of a winter coat when the summer sun shone. There was, however, time freed up from no longer having to apply make-up or spend time in grooming her long dark hair, no time wasted on searching through a wardrobe full of clothes. She did not miss any of it and it only made her smile to think of the futility of vanity, her inward beauty now outwardly shining, with more lustre than any lipstick could ever give. For the next seven years 'Satsangi', as her guru would call her, worked tirelessly, with total conviction, to accomplish all that was asked of her and what she asked of herself too.

Swami Satsangi read avidly into the night, the little rest she may have had after her daily chores happily sacrificed to gain deeper insights into the esoteric world that was her new reality. Her literary past encompassing the English classics – Austen, Brontë, Byron, Chaucer, Eliot, Huxley, Shakespeare – was now replaced with treatises of ancient and modern seers of philosophy. The concepts she encountered in these unfamiliar, complex texts slipped easily into her mind, these books somehow neither strange nor contradictory to her way of thinking. Instead, she felt inspired and encouraged, as if these insights had only temporarily been covered up by the maya that had been her childhood life, still residing in her deeper psyche, timely reminders rather than concepts to be absorbed and understood for the first time. Within just two short years Swami Satsangi turned this refreshed bank of knowledge into her own authored works, books that turned complex matters into easily readable formats that would help the uninitiated to move quickly to deeper levels of understanding. Besides her reading, writing and daily chores, she was also often attentively by her guru's side on his gruelling travel programme to places like Brisbane, Colombo, London, Melbourne, Paris... her busy schedule relentless.

As seven years passed, a strong bond was firmly established between these two remarkable people – Swami Satsangi, the devout disciple, and her beloved guru. She never had to question anything she was instructed to do. Swami Satyananda continued to be the driving force for her and the other disciples whom he would guide according to their abilities. He always seemed to know exactly what was right for anyone at a given point in time. Swami Satyananda, in actuality, was always a disciple at heart himself, ever true to the teachings of his own guru.

But there is no doubt that the guru–disciple relationship that Swami Satyananda and Swami Satsangi shared was truly profound. Their bond meant that for several years they would work in absolute harmony together to achieve what neither of them could possibly have done on their own. There was no need for them to sit together, discuss things at length, create detailed plans to be followed through, for their relationship was not set in a typically mundane or ordinary existence. Swami Satsangi and her guru communicated on a quite different plane – what one thought the other enacted, what one felt the other also felt. This was a union of two people, not on any physical level but a commingling of two intertwined spirits brought together to create a powerful force.

The energy force that the guru and disciple invoked could only be described as *'Shakti Manifest'*, the pure consciousness of Lord Shiva made manifest by the explosive energy of Goddess Shakti.

Samadhi

Given the evident close guru-disciple bond that Swami Satyananda and Swami Satsangi had developed between them, it was not at all surprising to anyone that it was Swami Satsangi who accompanied Swami Satyananda for a major part of his journey when he renounced all that he had and left the Munger ashram behind. Neither was it surprising that it was Swami Satsangi who was at his side when he embarked on the Rikhia phase of his life.

Life at Rikhia, once established, continued without too much complication, with hard work and austerities the order of the day, but contentedly and ceaselessly embracing a life of spiritual fulfilment. We have witnessed already a few of the changes that were initiated in the lives of so many there.

Swami Satyananda had initiated Swami Satsangi into the rites of Paramhansa in 2007, a status that a woman *sannyasin* could rarely attain, a stage in life where someone is recognised as having reached the ultimate, supreme way of being, transcended everyday consciousness, and achieved final beatitude.

No one really wanted the patterned way of living at Rikhia to change. In this life of relative serenity, Swami Satyananda no longer needed to traverse the globe. Swami Niranjan, his accomplished successor at Munger, was ably tending to the needs of the sea of Satyananda followers from across the globe. Swami Satsangi was clearly spiritually developed to the point where her status as a Paramhansa was irrefutable. However, Swami Satsangi's elevation should perhaps have been a signal to people that things were about to change.

On 5 December 2009, both Swami Niranjan at the ashram in Munger and Swami Satsangi in Rikhia were restless, and unusually for them, they found themselves unable to fully concentrate on the ceaseless number of duties that they had intended to accomplish that day. At ten o'clock that night, Swami Satyananda summoned Swami Satsangi to his side. This was the moment that she was to learn that her 'comfortable' existence was about to change – dramatically. Still restless as she approached her guru, she found him sitting relaxed in his usual meditative pose. In a calm and composed manner, he quite simply told her:

'I have received my return ticket and I have to leave now.'

'How will you leave? Where are you going?' Swami Satsangi asked.

He replied in Hindi, '*Ticket aa gaya, ham ja rahe hain*' (The ticket has come, I'm going).

The departure from life in this manner is only possible by a 'realised soul' when one has attained *samadhi*, when meditation practices have culminated to a point at which the mind has revealed itself to itself, only knowledge, intelligence continues to exist, no further dissipation is possible in such a being. This rare state is only reached by the extraordinary few – quite understandably, not many would ever have the courage to end their lives in such a manner. Tired of his aging physical body, though at eighty-six years still a very active and fit man, Swami Satyananda's physical abilities were constrained compared to the energetic days of his youth. He felt the end of his life was drawing near. He told his disciples that he knew the time for him to leave his earthly body was coming soon. But, knowing that he still had dharma, duties, to fulfil, he needed to know that he could return again one day in human form. Many times Swami Satyananda had said:

> I am waiting to leave this body, but I am not going until I get my return ticket. I do not want emancipation, *moksha*, or any personal satisfaction which comes with spiritual enlightenment. My aim and aspiration in this life and in all future lives is to help others. To wipe the tears of suffering and pain from the eyes of every person who is seeking solace, peace, plenty and prosperity. That is the only purpose of my life.

News of a 'return ticket' had come to him on that day and he prepared immediately to curtail his current earthly existence, the particular 'astrological conjunction' only a twenty-minute window of opportunity. This news was delivered to Swami Satsangi just as matter-of-factly as he had delivered the news of his departure from Munger to Swami Niranjan some twenty years before.

Swami Satsangi was aghast. She knew that there was something strange about the day, but this was totally unexpected news. She knew also that there was absolutely nothing at all that could be done that would make her beloved guru withdraw from his intended course – any attempt to change his mind would be utterly futile. Totally unattached to material matters, Swami Satyananda maintained his self-composure as if he was merely planning to go on a short trip, to return just a few days later.

At ten minutes before midnight, a few of the ashram disciples gathered together. Ganga *jal,* water from the Ganga, and tulsi leaves were requested to be brought to the room where Swami Satyananda calmly sat.

With tulsi leaves in his mouth he drank the sacred water. After chanting his guru mantra, he joined his hands in *pranam mudra,* in prayer pose.

Bhagavan, ham taiyaar hain, ham ko le chalo

Lord, I am ready. Take me now.

Chanting Om three times, he was gone.

Now at one with the cosmic consciousness…

The disciples could only look on in bewilderment at the scene that passed before their very eyes, lasting only a few moments but for a seemingly endless duration. They had intellectually understood that Swami Satyananda would leave the earth behind one day at a time of his choosing, but to see this resolve enacted without any hint of drama in front of their very eyes was a somewhat different matter, quite impossible to immediately absorb and understand.

Devout disciples, they were unattached to all that was earthly, but still, human after all, they struggled to keep their composure. When the message of Swami Satyananda's intended departure had been given to Swami Satsangi, she had contacted her *guru bhai*, Swami Niranjan. Distraught also, he arrived in Rikhia to find Swami Satyananda had already left his earthly body. Fully knowing that Swami Niranjan was the only person who may just possibly have been able to have circumvent this unexpected and extraordinary turn of events, Swami Satyananda had deliberately timed his final act in this life to ensure that he and Swami Niranjan would not be in each other's presence for his few last moments on earth.

As preparations for the funeral rites went on through the night, news of Swami Satyananda's sudden departure was already spreading and by five o'clock the next morning, people had started to arrive to say their final farewells to Swami Satyananda. People paid their last respects and received a final *darshan*, blessings, from their guru. His body was still upright and seated in the lotus position, his composure evident even then.

Swami Satyananda had fulfilled all the duties that he had been compelled to do in this life and had left comfortable in the knowledge that his teachings would be continued by his two foremost successors.

> *My wishes have all matured*
> *And I have written the whole song.*
>
> *Today my songs rise*
> *From all directions of the world*

And in the limelight

Of the moon and the stars

Flows the light of your prana.

All the Vedas have been sung

And all the shastras *have been written.*

Today I have given the prana

Of my jnana *to all.*

And I have already given you everything

In the form of two beautiful flowers.

Swami Satyananda

As the crowds dispersed from Rikhia, Swami Satsangi began to absorb the reality of her new circumstances. The man she had first met some forty years earlier, the guru under whose tutelage she had blossomed for almost thirty years, was suddenly no longer physically present in her midst.

But she had enormous duties to carry out. She could not afford the luxury of mourning or dwell on what was undoubtedly an enormous loss. She had to keep on going, to muster together the strength that had placed her in her current role as a *Paramhansa* and *acharya* of Rikhiapeeth. She continued to shoulder all her responsibilities stoically. Outwardly, she had accepted the circumstances as they were, but inwardly she dearly missed the embodied presence of someone who was in effect a part of herself, her consciousness, always there to guide her and give her moral strength in each and every one of her actions.

Paramhansa

Just as anyone who has borne the loss of a loved one knows only too well, though the heartache felt only gradually subsides, life all around continues as it was before – your pain is yours only and Swami Satsangi was no exception in this regard. She grew naturally into the life of a Paramhansa and so also Rikhia continued to grow. The local communities have continued to thrive and become self-sustaining. They are still well supported by the ashram, but in a more targeted way to meet their ever more sophisticated needs.

The ashram infrastructure has grown remarkably to support the continuously increasing number of visitors who attend the multifarious programmes that are more extensive and adventurous year after year. Many thousands now regularly pass through the ashram gates to partake in these high-quality, informative and often life-changing events, all undertaken in most pleasant surroundings. The now teenage *kanya*s, the young girls who were early initiators of change, are in charge of many of the programmes that take place in Rikhia, their confidence and stature belying their young age.

Swami Satsangi had began travelling again for some years. Considered a guru by the huge number of aspiring yogis that she herself has initiated into this lineage of yoga; she sees herself, however, first and foremost as her guru's disciple, intent on carrying on the work that he had begun. I had the good fortune to be in Australia in March 2013 when Swami Satsangi visited there – she had come all the way from Rikhia just to be at the Satyananda ashram near Melbourne to celebrate the Easter weekend with the disciples there. This was a poignant occasion for her, returning exactly thirty years after accompanying Swami Satyananda there, an emotional time for all present as she was welcomed back as the guru rather than the young 'Satsangi' at the outset of her new life as a *sannyasin*.

The Rocklyn ashram is located in the outskirts of Melbourne in a beautiful forest. The way of life, is in many ways, a carbon copy of the Rikhia ashram, with the traditional chanting, the ritual *havans*, the many discourses all running to precision-timing. Accommodation is efficiently organised, the considerable overspill of people arriving for this momentous occasion housed in well-equipped tents or transported to the nearby Melbourne University halls of residence; many others brought their own camping equipment, self-sufficient in the extensive ashram grounds. Breakfast, lunches and dinners were served to exact timing, bountiful and delicious vegetarian meals, alternatives even given to cater to the growing numbers of wheat-, gluten- and lactose-intolerant people of the twenty-first century!

As a pleasant aside, I was quite excited to see, for the first time in my life, the indigenous kangaroos each day as I regularly walked around the beautiful surrounding area during the breaks from the busy schedule. On most of these walks I was accompanied by a variety of people who had travelled to Melbourne for the occasion – some had been visiting the ashram for thirty years, some for just a few; many had also visited the Satyananda ashrams in India.

The majority of people I interacted with were trained Satyananda yoga teachers, not a vocation that they made a living from, but more often a discipline they felt compelled to share their knowledge of. Many of them were already in the caring professions – doctors, nurses, researchers and others. Most had not specifically chosen this particular 'brand' of yoga, rather, it had chosen them – a chance encounter, a casual acquaintance, or a spare and spontaneous moment in time had led them to one of the many programmes conducted at Rocklyn or elsewhere in Australia. But they all consistently agreed that once that spark was ignited, when that initial contact had been established, something inside them knew that this particular form of yoga was the path of self-fulfilment intended for them.

As the programmes got underway, everyone listened intently to Swami Satsangi as she delivered several messages to the hundreds of people gathered there from all over Australia. One of her talks focused on sharing the developments that Rikhia had undergone in the twenty-plus years of her stay there. She spoke about empowerment and the necessity to help people to look after themselves as they had done in Rikhia, she described how even the children there were now empowered to live a life of dignity with courage and confidence.

Swami Satsangi openly confided that in the early days of Rikhia, she had not always agreed with Swami Satyananda's philosophies of empowering these people. She recounted a particular occasion from a day in the past. As she was somewhat begrudgingly sorting out a consignment of clothes and other goods that had been sent to the ashram from Singapore, her mind had been preoccupied with the thought that she did not want to spend her time on such tasks. She felt that she did not want to be involved in giving charity, this was not what she was in the ashram for. What could she possibly learn from such mundane chores? She was deep in thought when Swami Satyananda, as if reading her mind, unexpectedly appeared in front of her. Patiently, he told her that this work would earn her merit when she had to confront God. It was not writing books, giving lectures and seminars that would see her progress in her spiritual aspirations, rather it was selfless service in helping others that would enable her to understand the true meaning of peace and harmony. She readily saw the wisdom of his words and this acceptance was cemented by the evident results of how their hard labour in those early days fructified to make Rikhia the place that it is today.

But the topic that featured most in Swami Satsangi's talks to the people gathered together near Melbourne was love.

The festival of Holi in India appears to the uninitiated as a day of great merriment when with gay abandon people plaster each other with copious amounts of colourful powder. And indeed, that is the outward manifestation of this occasion. The Holi festival also falls close to Easter, usually some time in March, marking the end of the cold north Indian winter – it is primarily a day intended as an expression of unity, love and harmony, a day when all divisions between people are set aside in a sort of 'temporary amnesty'.

Swami Satsangi told the audience that, as she sat in meditation on the day of Holi in 2010, three months after she had witnessed her guru's departure from his body, he suddenly appeared in a vision before her. He then gave her the message that:

> *Love is the most important thing; there is nothing more important than love. Love is truth and love is God. There is no difference between God and love.*

Though life at Rikhia was certainly much more focused on divine and heavenly realms than life at Munger had been, a shift in emphasis was evident in the many manifestations of 'gods' on display and the focus on worship and prayer, service and love rather than yoga. The real significance of this had not readily sunk into the minds of the people at Rikhia – people knew it was 'different' but how it was so was not easily explicable. But from the moment that Swami Satsangi had this vision of her guru during that particular Holi festival, she was transfixed. 'Talk' of love was no longer mere words. She told her audience how:

> It became an experience. I began experiencing it. And that changed my perception of everything… everything appeared different. The same trees appeared different, the birds were

different, the people looked different, and the smiles too looked different. Absolutely everything appeared different. When one experiences 'Love', in the true sense of the word, then the whole world appears different. It's like when we find ourselves in love with someone for the first time, everything around us and everything in us changes. It's something close to that... probably much more than that. A big transformation. When we think of transformation, then we have to start thinking on these lines. How can we transform to that extent where we can experience that state of bliss and love. This is the message of Holi... Love each other. On that day, everyone forgets their grievances. Even the bitterest enemies forget the past and hug each other. You decide to stop brooding over the past and move on.

During the few short days that the people of Australia spent together with Swami Satsangi during these Easter celebrations, there was certainly an outpouring of love for her. The third and last day of her visit culminated in around two hundred yoga aspirants being initiated into varying stages in their personal journeys of transformation, a ceremony not entirely dissimilar to a first communion of the Catholic church, though a ceremony based on a well-considered personal choice, generally at a more mature point of life rather than a hereditary custom. It was such a pleasure to witness their beaming faces as they exited from this ceremony on that final day, those in attendance having had the rare opportunity of receiving, firsthand, blessings from Swami Satsangi.

I left Melbourne and the Rocklyn ashram after just four short days that Easter weekend. It was a magical time that seemed to go on forever, immersed as we were in the serene atmosphere of positive energy. Swami Atmamuktananda, the head of this ashram, like Swami Satsangi, is a formidable but gentle and loving woman dedicated to serving others. She would rightly be proud of the success these few days had been.

I left Australia with many lasting impressions of the wondrous powers of yoga. The most moving story I heard though was from a ten-year-old boy I met one day while I was walking alone in the forest. Deep in thought, contemplating on all that I had been observing and feeling during my visit, this young boy suddenly appeared at my side. Confidently striking up a conversation and accompanying me for the rest of the way, he told me how he was visiting the ashram with his mother and sister. In the short time that we spent together that day he told me how yoga had helped him come to terms with his parents' separation, how it had helped him concentrate on his studies and to excel in sports such as the high jump and running. He told me how his mother was reluctant to let him get formally 'initiated' into yoga practices, feeling he was too young to be given his own mantra to chant. However, this young boy was so sure of himself and what he wanted to do that he personally sought an audience with Swami Satsangi to enlist her in supporting his case. His face was the perfect picture of happiness amongst the crowd that emerged from the ceremony that day, this young boy, mature beyond his years, but a fun-loving and innocent child too. I was deeply touched when he came out of this ceremony and immediately walked over to tell me about his feelings at that moment.

Combining all that I found at this gathering with the impressions now firmly marked in my mind from the number of visits I have had the opportunity to make to Rikhia, I left Australia with the realisation that, while Swami Satsangi is absolutely accepted by all as 'the guru', as opposed to the messenger of the guru, she is in reality – as I deeply feel – an embodiment of Swami Satyananda. Her talks, her actions are to me so vividly entangled with her guru's words that I cannot determine where Swami Satyananda ends or where Swami Satsangi begins. Though physically gone from this earth, Swami Satyananda is in communication with Swami Satsangi just as he was before his sudden and unusual departure in circumstances too surreal for our ordinary minds to comprehend.

Swami Satsangi, for me, is the living evidence of what can be accomplished when the Shiva and Shakti elements of two superconscious beings unite. In essence, Swami Satsangi and Swami Satyananda are one, just as Shakti and Shiva are one. Swami Satyananda's greatest accomplishments during his eighty-six years, I believe, occurred in the last twenty years of his life in Rikhia with the manifestation of Shakti's unparalleled energy. But what was achieved there could not have been done without his 'other half'. To manifest what was in Swami Satyananda's consciousness required the unbounded energy of Swami Satsangi, a woman in the forefront of the flowering of this rural area. Its inhabitants benefited from the joint efforts of these two intertwined people.

When sannyasa *blooms*
And knowledge dawns
And power unfolds,
It sanctifies history and posterity.
One single sannyasin
Can be the creator of an epoch,
A seer of intuition
And a mastermind of tradition.

Swami Satyananda Saraswati

Search for Freedom

Though we are witnesses to the fact that only the very few gems of humanity reach to the level of development such as Swami Satyananda managed to do in his lifetime, we are also acutely aware, but somehow choose to ignore, that deep-rooted in the heart of every single human being on this earth is the desire to know one's self, to understand who we are and what we are here for. At some point in all of our lives, something will trigger us to think beyond our material world, to go beyond what we see, feel, taste, touch and smell in our everyday level of 'operational consciousness'. We live an almost automated existence of thought and reaction, the two often confused with unpredictable moods and emotions we do not understand or know how to control. We oscillate continuously from love to hatred, pride to jealousy, anger to joy as our lives go fleeting past in the blink of an eye. The consequences of our uncontrolled and unpredictable ways of acting are evident for all to see in the never-ending cycle of violence, within and across nations, that continues unabated all around us.

We have scraped a tiny tip of a mammoth iceberg in this brief overview that only begins to touch on how, with the will and energy of just a very few people, a considerable upliftment could be brought about in the lives of so many, the thousands of people in a rural land who had very little hope of improving their lot. The small group of Swamis who took bold steps to make changes in their own lives and to serve the underprivileged of Rikhia are a shining example of what humankind can quite readily do. Although all the Swamis who now reside in Rikhia have an austere lifestyle, their own lives are enriched by the deep sense of fulfilment and joy that they experience every day as they witness firsthand the developments all around them.

Many visitors to the ashram have also given up their worldly comforts to live a basic existence for short periods of time. They participate in *seva* or attend a course or particular programme for a defined period of time. Later, they depart from the ashram with a deep sense of satisfaction after the experience of contributing to support the local community – whether they have been involved in assisting in the after-school classrooms teaching English, distributing the daily after-school meals, giving monthly pensions to the elderly of the community or any other service.

These experiences of supporting others in their time of need and seeing the benefits come to fruition, impact all of us in a similar manner. We derive a certain, undeniable pleasure from witnessing the joy of others, the positive atmosphere that pervades from undertaking selfless acts. But most of us return after these short sojourns back to our everyday lives to get caught up once again in the machinery of work, family, possessions, seeking for new outlets from which we can derive pleasure.

Deep down in our hearts and minds we are all searching for exactly the same things. We all need to feel secure and we all seek happiness. We want to do the right thing: we know absolutely and fundamentally what is right and what is wrong. We do not need laws to tell us that stealing, killing or lying are improper acts, yet they do take place. When we do wrong, we lose our tranquillity, we cannot feel secure or happy and what we are seeking seems unattainable. And so the search goes on, with continuously changing moments of feeling secure and happy, insecurity and unhappiness, unable to lift ourselves beyond the realms of our ordinary existences, unable to even come close to attaining *moksha,* super-consciousness, *samadhi* – whatever we name that yet unfelt state of ultimate freedom, no longer bound by the search for anything at all, at peace with ourselves.

But then we reach a point in our evolution when we come to the realisation that material, earthly pleasures, even the occasional feel-good visits to ashrams or other charitable pursuits, are only temporary in nature. We come to understand that we do not know ourselves, we do not know what makes us function, we do not know why it is that we get caught up in the treadmill of life, earning to buy a bigger car, more gold, better holidays. We are continuously binding ourselves in the forlorn expectation that we will derive more freedom, but only imprison ourselves further as we encumber ourselves with more material possessions to take care of, more 'leisurely pursuits' that also tie us down – we find ourselves unable to get out of the perpetuating cycle of our busy and energy-draining lives. Life goes on entangling us in this way until something sparks inside us, wakes us up, makes us see the futility of our vicious circle of existence. Usually a crisis, something unexpected, an event we cannot control, a life-changing experience will be a trigger point that will make us hear that inner voice crying out to us just to stop! Whether we refer to the likes of Maslow's hierarchy of needs, Jung's collective consciousness or individuation, the dark night of the soul, Eastern or Western philosophers, ancient or modern philosophies... all are testaments to the fact of the unavoidable evolution of our species. This chain of events is as inherent in our nature just as the inherent nature of a seed is to bear fruit or flowers or whatever its destiny is intended to be. The final outcome is not optional.

> You are neither this body nor the mind. the Self is above and beyond the senses, intellect and physical consciousness. That is you.

All too often though, when at first we begin to awaken to the sad fact of our wasted lives, when the trigger point comes and creates a disturbance in our everyday existence, we just do not know what to do next. We become restless, anxious, ill at ease for reasons unfathomable. Acquaintances will brush our emotions off as temporary moodiness that will pass us by, a brief midlife crisis that will soon disappear before we return to our 'normal' selves. Opportunities are too often missed, perhaps exerting some change in direction but not on a personally beneficial trajectory, more one of appeasing our social interactions and obligations. Or we recognise the call but merely begin to intellectualise about concepts of self-realisation, have interesting conversations on the notions that we are not isolated islands of individuality, intended only to derive personal and temporary pleasures. Then we continue on as usual in our limited spheres of existence, unable to summon up the courage to step outside our cloistered comfort zones.

Recognition of this natural craving, the instinctive awakening to our inner voice is today a far more widely recognised phenomenon, as more and more of us are free to take proper cognisance of this than we have ever been able to do in the past. The industrialisation of the last century has provided many with the luxurious opportunity for inner reflection amidst the clamouring outcries against the denaturing of our planet. Maslow and others of his time attributed only one or two per cent of the human population with being developed enough to recognise this natural tendency to develop their latent potentiality – but the numbers of such people is on the increase. This is clearly evidenced by the countless number of yoga retreats, personal development books, life-changing workshops, an endless list of opportunities unfolding to aid us on our personal journeys. As Jung asserted, the *collective consciousness,* the more widely held shared beliefs and ideals that we hold about our species are attuning us to the fact that we need to move forward towards an alternative lifestyle, imbibing strong moral attitudes and shared responsibility to ensure a better environment for all on this earth, restricted no longer just to the fortunate few. We cannot continue only to read, attend workshops, watch 'YouTube' videos and then go about our daily lives as we have been doing for the centuries that have already passed us by. It is quite evident to all of us that we cannot continue to live this way today. We live in a brutal world, an existence where the downtrodden of one group are the perpetrators of harm also to others, finally injurious to those that are the very basis of society, denigrating the very givers of life, the mothers and daughters, many with no platform from which to raise their own voices.

Humankind has to evolve. Transformation is a scientific fact. It is not a philosophy, faith or creed. The path of transformation and evolution gives meaning to life. You cannot deny evolution.

What has happened in Rikhia over the last two and a half decades has so clearly demonstrated in a low-key, simple way how society as a whole can benefit when we move away from merely thinking and talking about what we all know to be the truth of how we should live our lives and actually begin to take some personal accountability for initiating action. But it is clear also that we cannot really help others in an effective and sustainable manner if we do not first help ourselves to move away from our conditioned way of reacting to situations that transpire all around us. The Swamis who triggered the changes at Rikhia were already far more developed in their understanding of human potential. With their levels of consciousness at an already heightened state, they were adequately equipped to act as role models to be emulated. They already knew, without a single trace of doubt, the absurdity of the trappings of our materially inclined modes of operation. This small group of Swamis could already identify with the enlightened words of the Dalai Lama when asked what surprised him most about humanity:

> Man. Because he sacrifices his health in order to make money. Then he sacrifices money to recuperate his health. And then he is so anxious about the future that he does not enjoy the present; the result being that he does not live in the present or the future; he lives as if he is never going to die and then dies having never really lived.

But amidst all the, perhaps confusing, plethora of life-altering opportunities, the question is: where to start? How do we get ourselves onto the right path? How will we know we are heading in the right direction? Our inherent nature is to develop our consciousness to a higher level. Intellectually, we fully understand that we are destined for far greater things than the severely limited usage of our infinite potential presently allows. But our conditioned upbringing, the lives that most of us have led up to now have also ingrained in us a natural tendency to seek security, to covet love and attention from others to whom we turn to for the assurance of our own personal worth. But how can we break out of these cycles of dependency and insecurity, the fear of loneliness, that has been the norm for our species for millennia?

Your vision will become clear only when you look into your heart. Who looks outside, dreams. Who looks inside, awakens.

Carl Gustav Jung

But we have to take the first step towards a new way of living; a new approach to enable us to reach our potential. Continuing to live our lives as we have always done can only result in the same consequences that we have become so accustomed to expect. The vast majority of us leave this organic matter in which our true selves currently reside, this body that will wither away when we have breathed our last, departing without any understanding of what our lives were about. Then, ultimately, we end up achieving nothing at all. No legacy, no long-lasting impressions left behind, to comfort those who bid us farewell

Change of any magnitude requires an immense effort, a mindset shift, discovery of a profundity too compelling to be ignored, with an impact that the likes of Einstein's theories of relativity had on our interpretation of life. Understanding our own minds, our inner beings also requires a certain amount of 'applied science', a complex process of turning our own mind towards understanding itself. It is, in effect, an oxymoron, a contradiction of terms, a seemingly impossible ask of our limited selves. But there is a science that has stood the test of time to deal with such dilemmas of man. The science of yoga, the bringing together of body, mind and soul into a single, harmonious state; yoga is a tried and tested applied science to help us find the way to turn the mind in on itself. Yoga far surpasses the commonly held belief that it is an alternative exercise regime. While it is true that it has a physical element, it is so intricately researched that it can enable the optimisation of our health, our wellbeing a prerequisite for an arduous journey to the self within. This complete science of humanity simply termed as 'yoga' shows us many paths that accommodate all possible human archetypes. It is one of the best methods to ultimately equip ourselves for this task of knowing and realising our inner selves. But...

Nothing happens until something moves.

Albert Einstein

Yoga, this most complex of sciences, has many facets and proponents advising multiple variations and methods of practice. Initially though, all we essentially have to do is watch the movement of our breath. Breath is our vital life force moving in and out of our nostrils to our lungs some 21,600 times each and every day. Moving in and moving out, our lungs expand and contract this number of times to ensure oxygen is carried efficiently through our bloodstream to maintain the functioning of our vital organs, ensuring the oxygenation of all the millions of cells and tissues of our bodies. Yet we hardly notice it all. The process of breathing continues on its own while we go about our daily business. On and on it goes, in and out, in and out. Yet if breathing stops, just for one or two minutes, our lives in this current state of vibration, would come to an abrupt end. Any change, large or small and for whatever reason, in the state of our emotions will cause a change in the rate and rhythm of our breath, yet still we are oblivious to this fact. When we are angry, our breath becomes faster; afraid, it draws up deep in our throat; asleep, quite shallow. On and on it goes.

Yet in effect, it is our very breath that controls our lives as it constantly changes its pattern in reaction to these variations in our uncontrolled emotions – one moment sad, the next moment happy. If only we would start to control our breath, we would be in control of our emotions, in control of ourselves and of our lives. We can set ourselves free from our conditioned way of reacting to situations. We can set ourselves free from the suppressed memories of our past tucked conveniently out of reach in the deep subconscious of our mind. And thus we can be free to act in harmony with our thoughts. We can stop merely intellectualising theories and actually act according to what we know to be correct. We can stop reacting to situations in our old habitual and customised ways. Solutions to the many dilemmas we face and the struggle to see a way out will easily be determined. Through the practice of yoga we can readily bring about a state of total harmony between our minds and bodies, no more the tortuous confusions of thinking right, but doing wrong. Those internal fights that can never be won, these battles with our own minds, they can come to an end, this roller-coaster of emotions can stop. Just simply by breathing, by becoming aware of a phenomenon that we cannot survive without, all disharmony in our lives will naturally, gradually, come to an end and we will find peace within ourselves.

The ancient yogic science that can teach us all about the

breath is known as Swara Yoga, the study of the continuous flow of air through the nostrils, a systematic approach to studying and then controlling the breath. Understanding how our breath is affected by the phases of the moon and the sun, how the forces of nature impact everything on the planet, night and day, birth and death, the changing seasons, tidal patterns... but to begin with, with no instruction, right away, all we need do is simply sit quietly and watch this rhythmic flow. For a few minutes a day, while we walk, or while we drive, a ride on the train or the bus at any time, day or night, and in any place, we can just quietly stop the chattering thoughts of our minds and watch our breath. As this is done, gradually, the changes will come. Naturally, we will want to know more, do more, repeat the concentration on breath and in this way, the right connections will automatically happen on their own, effortlessly.

As we bring harmony back into our lives, return to the unconditioned state of mind that we were born with but have temporarily forgotten, we will begin to realise that there is nothing we cannot achieve. We make our own realities as we reach that point of development, that superconscious state that we are all intended to achieve. Ultimately, the mind can achieve anything that it chooses to think about. Not only yoga testifies to this, but so do the growing number of scientists exploring quantum physics as they explore their ideas together with great minds such as the Dalai Lama's.

As we come to understand the immense powers that we all innately have, we can all contribute to the betterment of the world in which we live, just as Swami Satsangi and her fellow Swamis continue unselfishly to do each and every single day of their lives.

> Man is destined to awaken... at some point of evolution, even if no conscious effort is made to liberate the energy and expand the awareness. This is the natural heritage and birthright of every human being, but without applying a specific procedure it will take a long, long time. The practices of [yoga] hasten the natural process of evolution and allow that experience to unfold in this life itself, here and now, at this very moment. This experience bestows *ananda* and *jnana*, bliss and knowledge, which man seeks through external objects, but never finds. On account of this, human life is full of misery, frustration and depression. The experience that arises through expansion of consciousness and liberation of energy is the only permanent solution to human suffering.
>
> Swami Satyasangananda Saraswati, 2008, p. 10

Moving On

Many of the seekers amongst the few that are fortunate enough to get that inner spark that drives us to more intimately know our own selves somehow or other find themselves at the gates of the Satyananda Rikhia ashram, the place where for more than thirty years of Swami Satsangi's life as a *sannyasin* have now passed, a life dedicated to serving the needy in body and mind, a service that the vast majority of us are in desperate need of. There are no days off in this life, no weekends, no summer or winter breaks. Although she has reached her sixtieth year, there are no retirement plans for Swami Satsangi, no pension packages, no savings in the bank and certainly no leisurely holiday cruises.

Waking by three o'clock each morning, Swami Satsangi begins the day performing her own personal *sadhana*, her own esoteric practices; though she may appear entirely accomplished to all who know her, she continuously strives for further perfection. By five o'clock, the ashram is alive as the Swamis gather together for early morning chanting and worship to be joined at six by the usually large contingent of visitors. Breakfast is at seven, classes or other group sessions commence thereafter, followed by periods of *seva*, lunch, more classes, dinner, evening programmes. By eight in the evening, the visitors are in their accommodation, exhausted, lights out, sleeping early in readiness for another busy day ahead. Work, however, continues for the *sannyasin*s who remain busy, preparing for the days that follow. No stone is left unturned to ensure that, as always, everything runs smoothly no matter what the activity; events will all appear to flow seamlessly by the participants. All day long, people vie with others for an opportunity to meet Swami Satsangi, to seek advice on a vast range of topics: marriage decisions, business problems, health matters, relationship matters, (sometimes) spiritual questions, personal *sadhana*... anything under the sun will be asked of her just as she witnessed her own parents posing such question to her own family guruji in the past. Swami Satsangi will spend hours every day patiently listening and guiding people in resolving their many issues. Though much of what people ask may seem trifling, of little import, the guru's guidance gives a certain confidence, an inner contentment at confiding personal concerns, even though they may choose not to act on the advice given. Nonetheless, there is no doubt that hearing the guru's words of wisdom is considered time valuably spent, a release from the, most often, unnecessary, stressful turmoil that we allow into our lives.

But one day, Swami Satsangi will move on. Like all of us,

at some point, she will have to drop this mortal body. That day is not yet known to us. Swami Satsangi, however, has been withstanding the most demanding of *sadhana* practices – *panchagni* (five fires) *sadhana* – an ancient ritual that has been undertaken by very few people, prescribed only for *Paramhansa sannyasins* such as her guru, a practice undertaken to experience the deepest inner purity. Swami Satyananda undertook this most arduous of all yogic *sadhanas* over a period of nine years in isolation, surrounded by four burning fires, one each in the north, the south, the east and the west, the fifth being the hot summer sun overhead. The ability to maintain such forbearance while concentrating on the ritual chantings to be completed a precise number of times, and keeping to the order of the herbs, flowers and oils to be ceremoniously poured into the fire, is no easy matter. All the while, the burning flames surround a lone body and soul, unassisted in the centre of it all.

Swami Satsangi has spoken of the energising effects that this practice has had on her, not the difficulties she withstood while doing it. She hadn't realised how much she had absorbed of this *sadhana* as she had observed Swami Satyananda endure these austere practices in the past. For the past two years now, Swami Satsangi has undertaken this *sadhana,* perhaps a signal to us that we may see this guru gradually withdraw from public life in the not-too-distant future as she surely must do one day.

Swami Satsangi has no personal desires in this life – she does not seek any rewards, no recognition for the work she tirelessly does throughout weeks, months, the changing seasons and the countless years. Her only desire is to be reunited with her guru, to walk more closely in his shadow once more, to start over again, perhaps to create more Rikhias.

I have had the amazing good fortune to spend many hours in conversation with her, time spent in awe listening to what she has told me of her life. To hear her tell of her experiences firsthand has been an honour that I would never have believed could happen in my life. As I have come to know her just a little, I have thought of her almost unceasingly. When I researched and thought about her life, my respect and admiration for her has grown exponentially. I cannot adequately describe the love, the waves of emotion that now flow within me if I catch even a glimpse of her or if I receive a mail or any form of contact is made.

As I have had this opportunity, I think it fitting to share some of Swami Satsangi's own words here to convey points about her life and where it will now go, clearly more beautifully spoken than my words could ever do. What follows is a conversation we had together in May 2013... for anyone who has had the good fortune to have heard Swami Satsangi speak, you will know you can lose yourself in her words. Close your eyes, imagine, then feel her calm, beautiful voice floating dreamily around you...

～

Swami Satsangi (SS): 'When I had first decided to come to the ashram, it was Munger that I went to. This was at a time when the place was much smaller, an intimate place with a sort of homely, family atmosphere, even Ganga Darshan was not built back then, just a really small place with virtually nothing much there at all.

'I went to the ashram without any ambition of achieving anything at all in particular, it wasn't anything like that. And certainly I didn't go there with the thought that one day I would be some sort of senior figure in what was then to me a mysterious, but wondrous world, far removed from the relatively cosseted existence of my past. No, I really had no thought about becoming anything at all. I was not even concerned about taking *sannyas*, though that was certainly an aspect of this new life that had fascinated me as a child, the atmosphere with all these people in orange clothes, the smell of incense, the peace, all my senses I remember being bombarded on that very first day I visited there as a child. I really just wanted to be there in this magical atmosphere, to be a sincere disciple to the Guru who had somehow triggered something in me that I just could not possibly ignore. I just had to act on the feelings that were gnawing at me deep down in my soul, creating a restlessness that I just didn't comprehend really.

'The basis of discipleship, I somehow knew, was not yoga, it was not spirituality, it wasn't meditation, nor was it learning how to do anything. The basis of discipleship rather, I sensed, was one of surrender and faith. Not a blind faith, but a faith born out of total conviction, a sort of faith that seemed so very natural, so right for me. It was a feeling so strong, like a wave that had washed everything else out of my life. This faith alone, the conviction that I was doing what I was somehow meant to do, this was the sole motivating factor that compelled me way back then, as a young woman, to come to the ashram.

'With conviction such as this, transformation quite literally happens on its own. If I am transformed, then I don't know it. I don't know if I am changing. If I am becoming better or worse, I don't know it. I am living my life naturally, in the spirit of faith and surrender, no expectations of anything from anyone. There is so much power in faith and surrender that it automatically transforms you, you begin to see things differently, you have a different experience, you begin to think and respond differently. And that is what happened in my life.

'Usually what happens, however, is you meet a person whom you think is your guru, you have a liking for that person and as you come to know this person more, that liking develops into love and affection, a love not in any worldly sense but a love of such high regard and respect for someone that you want to be the best that you can possibly be in their eyes – no amount of effort or sacrifice is ever too much. That's how it happens with most people, a gradual awakening process that moves you along in its evolutionary wake.

'For me, there was no gradual move from acceptance to reverence of my guru. Right from the beginning I had no doubts. I didn't go through this gradual phase of development, a process of initially liking my guru and over time, becoming more convinced that I was on the right path. For me, right from the beginning, all my focus, all my thoughts and awareness was directed towards my guru. My devotion was ever constant, never erratic, no oscillation at all in my mind. It was constant for all the years that I had the opportunity to be in his presence. And even now, though physically Paramhansaji is not present, in his absence it is still like this. That I had the blessing of such fortitude, such a steadfastness that enabled me to grow as I have grown, is not at all down to anything that I did. I don't take any credit for that because I didn't do anything for it. It just happened that way and I can only attribute this to the grace of my guru. He could bring that out from within me. So the total awareness of my guru was the only transformative factor in my life that had begun from the very first moment I had met him.

'Swami Satyananda used to say, "I don't have to tell Satsangi what I need and what to do – she knows beforehand. If I need a glass of water, she's there with the water, if I need something she's there with that. I don't need to speak to her, she just picks it up. She knows the requirement of that time. If the door needs to be opened, she does it, I don't need to tell her." This comes with total awareness because you are in sync. This is the rapport I had with Swami Satyananda – it was a very deep connection at some level where he used to think and I used to just act. Even now I experience that in my life. Even when he is not in the body, I can tap that. Many of the things that come to me, they are from him and I know that. Earlier, when he was around, I could always check if I was on the right track, now I have no way to do that, but still the feeling is that it is coming from him. So this is the main reason for the transformation, not the *sannyas*, not yoga... nothing of that. This is also true of Swami Satyananda in his life. The reason why he became what he became, was not yoga, it was not the ashram that he had built, it was this constant awareness of his guru, and that was natural for him as well.

'From the time when I actually saw him in my early years, the instruction which he gave me, that is what I followed in my life knowingly or unknowingly. Although later I lost touch with him, I followed only that pattern. And when I saw his picture again at a later age, it triggered off something again. Then when I came to the ashram, after that it was constant and total awareness, because then I was there all the time. When I was not with him then naturally, I had to do my job and do many things, so there was dissipation and a distraction, but at the back of my mind this was always there, that this is what I want to do, and how can I do it? There was no particular event or any vision, it was just being with him. When I took *sannyas* also, the ceremony which he conducted at my *sannyas* initiation, it was a very detailed and authentic ceremony, which is the traditional Virija Homa for *sannyasins*. The Virija Homa is a process that is performed according to ancient methods to a very precise detail that initiates a process deep within the individual where [s]he is reborn in the same body. When Swamiji initiated me into these ancient rites, I began to have new and quite profound insights – this was one particular moment in time where I could very readily discern a transformative effect in my life. In this traditional initiation ceremony, my last rites were performed and I literally felt myself stepping out of one existence and just naturally flowed into a new existence, a wonderful new life, a totally new and fresh beginning, but one consciously felt. Offering the *pinda daan*

to the ancestors, the offering to the gurus, were such profound
and very important moments in my life. The cords of my old
life were ceremoniously cut, the knots that may have bound
me to the past were once and for all completely severed and I
became a new person in the same body. The *sannyas* ceremony
that Swamiji conducted that day was a very important moment
for me, my surrender was total and complete. My new life was
sanctified and I just naturally flowed into this new beginning,
with no thoughts, no concerns, no anxiety at all about what
the future ahead may hold.

'And moving on, I never had any difficulty in *sannyas* life.
None. No mental, no emotional, no physical problems at all.
I just fitted in like it was the most natural thing for me. Not
that I had any difficulty in my earlier life – even there I was
totally at home and enjoying myself and everything, but when
I came here, life just seemed somehow much more natural,
like I had woken from a dream. I didn't feel like there was
anything I could not do; there was no awkwardness for me in
adjusting to a completely new way of living, a new way of being
in reality. Everything was just normal and natural. And that
is the way that one has to live the spiritual life. I can't pretend
to be something I'm not. I can pretend for maybe one day or
one month, but I can't pretend for a whole lifetime. After all,
what you are, you are. So that natural and spontaneous feeling
was very important for me. It was not contrived, I was not
trying to be something – I *was* that. And in that, the greatest
contributing factor was my guru. He gave me total trust and
faith. He didn't in any way mistrust or doubt me. He gave me

total trust to do what was needed for my growth. Of course he would correct me, but there was a bond of trust. When you receive trust from somebody, then something very special comes out. When you know that somebody trusts you and loves you as you are, not as they would like you to be, then the best in you comes out, something very creative comes out from within and you give everything to that. If you don't get love and trust, then everything gets suppressed. And this is true with everybody, not just with me.

'Even in family life, the children who get the love and trust of their parents or teachers and society, are more creative and expressive than others. The others may be creative and expressive, but they get suppressed. So I was very lucky that I got the total love and trust of my guru, which he gave to others as well, but that brought out the best in me, which perhaps until then was not getting expression. And that is the contributing factor to my transformation. In terms of my nature, I've always been like this. My natural tendencies were always to be very independent, to be quite fearless and confident in what I was doing. I had never felt that anything was impossible, right from childhood I was like that. But in childhood, of course, I didn't get the area of expression which I got here in the ashram. In Rikhia especially, I had a completely open field, and Swamiji always used to say, "It is by God's grace that you have been given this opportunity, nobody gets an opportunity to serve like this. It's hard to get a place to serve even if you want to. Even if you have that inner urge, you don't get a place for that. You really have to struggle to get a place and here you have all freedom to express that."

'So I would say that Swamiji used my nature to its optimum level. He even converted that part of my nature that could have created conflict. I wasn't perfect for sure, but he was able to use my imperfections in a constructive, positive way. With my sort of fearless, independent and "no care" attitude, I really could have had difficulties in a place such as Rihkia. But Swamiji, somehow he just knew how to use all our attributes in a way that was productive. I was so very fortunate in my life, quite literally I could say that lady luck had showered her blessings upon me. Luck, fate, destiny – they all played a very great part in the process of my transformation. Because even when you have the right place and the right person, when seemingly all the right ingredients are there, the outcome is not always as expected. I have seen this often, some people have all the opportunities, they have all the guidance, but still they are unable to take the leap that I was able to take. So that may have been my destiny as well. Swamiji was able to see that in this person, in me, that destiny was also favourable, so Swamiji's insights into what the future was to hold were critical in my future.

'Without a doubt, I had the best teacher; you couldn't get a better teacher than that. Swamiji was a person who truly understood the depth of someone's mind; he knew what exactly motivated someone and what their aims, their desires and their opportunities were. He had an insight into everything, so naturally he could trim and prune you in a way that was right just for you and give you the appropriate direction to set you on the right path. I saw him do this with so many people, not just with me. Everyone who came in contact with him, he uplifted and guided them; he gave people direction, a goal, an aim and a way to achieve these and move forward. Everyone that you see here… Swamiji was, and still is, in some way responsible for the way their lives have been shaped. All of us came to Swamiji at a very young age, not when we were elderly. In youth you have myriad problems, you don't understand anything, you glorify everything, and you are so idealistic. So you need a person who really is a master craftsman to be able to manage the different personalities, different egos, and different ways of thinking, different cultures and religions. And he was able to bring out the best in everyone.

'I was totally unskilled for the work which I had to do in the ashram. I didn't even know what a typewriter looked like, forget about typing. I had no knowledge of the scriptures because that was not my education. As an Indian, of course, I had some scant knowledge of yoga, but to the extent that I had practised some *asana*s. But there was absolutely no depth to my knowledge. I had no skills in management, I didn't know how to cook, and in fact I was a virtually useless person. To make a useless person like me useful, that was Swamiji's talent. Millions of useless people he has made useful. These are the contributing factors to my transformation. I was a person like anybody else, enjoying life, going to the restaurants, going to the discotheque, watching movies. I don't think I did anything useful in my life. I was just a body living my life and enjoying it, wasting time and wasting money. So to give such a person an aim, a goal and make that person feel the responsibility for that, make them work-oriented and selfless, that only a master craftsman can do. I was not selfless, I was a very selfish person, before I came to the ashram... I was living solely for myself.'

~

Barbara Pidgeon (BP): 'So what's next?'

SS: 'It's quite clear that Swamiji has created Rikhia as the public side of his mission, this is how spirituality has to express itself, there's no use saying "I'm spiritual" and not contributing to the world that you live in. So Rikhia is the public face of his mission. This has to grow and develop more. As far as Rikhia is concerned, the needs that were there when Swamiji arrived are not there today. And just yesterday I was thinking that ten years from now, how will Rikhia be? Today there are so many things here we could have never dreamed of. There is a cyber café, an alcohol shop here... I saw that board yesterday and I was shocked! There is a little restaurant which has opened where food is served, chow mein and things like that. There are two very big schools that have opened. So ten years from now, what will be the situation of Rikhia? The ashram has to evolve according to the needs of the people. They may not need what we are giving them now, they may not need education from us, or blankets and clothing and kitchenware, they may not need them. So what will they need? They may need peace of mind, they may need yoga, whatever they need, the ashram has to evolve along with Rikhia, that is quite clear. They may not even need a meal every day – they may come because they like to come, but they may not need it.

'From the beginning, the birth of Rikhia has been based on

whatever is the need of this place; accordingly, we have worked together to give the people help and address their immediate requirements. They don't need yoga right now, that is what Swamiji said. They need food, employment and shelter and medical assistance. That is how we started. Today they don't need shelter, so that we do on a small scale. Then education came up. Now tomorrow, if they won't need education from the ashram, if their needs are met through other means, then there would be no need for us to support them in this way. So it's very clear that Rikhia has to be a need-based evolution, we don't want to stagnate. The basis though, will always be spiritual, not material. And it has to evolve in the lines of the ashram tradition. Of course, although there is a tradition, there has to be a modern outlook which will have to be relevant to the day, so you can find a nice combination of tradition and modernity.

'Rikhia has to become an ashram with a tradition and a modern outlook, and also as a *tirtha*. A *tirtha* is a place where the energy is awakened, where there is a high level of energy, a positive and vibrant energy field that is spiritual in nature. And we have to continue to nurture the energy that Swamiji gave birth to here. He created this place as an ashram, not as an institution. Of course, it is registered and we have to follow the norms of an institution, but principally, Rikhia is an ashram committed to an ashram way of living. But it is this divine energy that is really the epicentre of all that has been created here. And without doubt, Rikhia has the potential to be at the heart of this energy, it has that potential. This is the place of Shakti, where she left her body, it is the Hridaya Peeth, so that factor will help the growth of Rikhia. And it is up to us to see that it is maintained according to the principles of such energetic forces, the undeniable magnetic forces that are discernibly present to anyone who visits this place.

'So this is the future of Rikhia. In that, the ashram and the *tirtha* concept of Rikhia, everything comes in... serve, love and give. The main factor is Swami Satyananda, because this is the link to him, for those who want to connect with him, because he left his body here. So one can say that Rikhia is the body of Swami Satyananda, where his heart beats. This is the heart centre of Swami Satyananda. He used to say, "I have a bank of hearts. You can leave your heart here, and I'll take very good care of it." Apart from the ashram and *tirtha,* this is the place of Swami Satyananda – he lived here, did *tapasya,* the *panchagni* and other austere practices that he underwent to burn away any trace of remaining impurities here, left his body here. To align with him, his teachings, his energy, to receive his grace and blessings and guidance... Rikhia has to develop as a place to connect with Swami Satyananda.

'Ashram, *tirtha* and Swami Satyananda – these are the three key characteristics of Rikhia, the three aspects that make it what it is. And within this setting we live our lives in accordance with our guru's *sankalpa*, the promise that he made to his own guru, to serve, love and give unconditionally and totally. This is how we live our lives here, and these will always be the guiding principles when we look after our neighbours, indiscriminately determined by the needs of the day.'

BP: 'Any specific plans for you personally?'

SS: 'I don't have any personal life. My life is an open book and it is a life totally dedicated to the furtherance of my guru's *sankalpa*, the resolution to serve, love and give that he also handed down to me. When I first came here, my life was, of course, very different to what it is today. Back then I used to do everything, I used to handle the keys, phones, guests, I could be seen from time to time driving a tractor around the grounds or riding a motorbike into Deoghar to get last-minute supplies. There was nothing I didn't do in those days – I was virtually running all the time and I was absolutely loving every minute of it. Then "this thing" got created. Before we realised it, this place we now so casually and fondly refer to as the Rikhia ashram, had sprung up almost without our noticing; we were just so busy all the time that it is only looking back now that we realise all that has taken place in such a relatively short period of time. Quite literally, Rikhia moved out of the dark ages into the current era in just a very few short years.

'So naturally, I have moved out of those early frenetic ways of operating, I'm out of that now and able to rely on others to take care of all these matters. Now I see myself much more like the guardian of all this, just teaching and training people. Now my role is much more focused in guiding the many aspirants who come here in spiritual matters; and I am still travelling to some extent, spreading the teachings of Swamiji and telling people about Rikhia – this is the main focus of my present role.

'And of course, I must focus on my own spiritual development, my own *sadhana* which I have to keep alive;

I have grown, of that there is no doubt, yet there is no end
to spiritual practice and I continue on this spiritual path
in accordance with the guidance that Swamiji gave me and
even today he is continuously guiding me in my spiritual
development.

'There are four key stages in the earthly life of a *sannyasa,*
this life of dedication and renunciation of all worldly affairs,
these four key points of evolution through *kutichaka, bahudaka,*
hansa and *paramhansa,* these four key steps in the Vedic, the
ancient, Indian concept of a full life, the evolving consciousness
of an awakened being through its various stages to that highest
possible stage of *ananda,* a state of ultimate bliss. As I continue
to grow, gradually I will more fully follow the lifestyle of a
Paramhansa, just as my guru lived. This is the path that I have
been initiated into and this is the path that I am ultimately
destined to follow. I will not be able to continue to do what I
do now for the rest of my life. Swamiji has shown me the way
– as he did, so too, I will gradually go into seclusion. Swamiji
clearly told me to "live in the world like a lotus flower so that
you're always pure and pristine, don't get soiled with the mud
that it lives in. And then when the time comes, extract yourself
out from that and continue with your journey. And one day,
merge into the absolute." This is my future.'

～

BP: 'Are you trying to find a successor?'
SS: 'At some time there will definitely be someone who will be
my successor. I cannot be here forever and definitely there has

to be somebody to continue this spiritual tradition. But I'm not over-focusing on that area, I feel that this is something which is predestined, God will determine who that person will be and when that person will be ready. You can't make successors, they come already with that potential and I need to recognise it. My role is only to recognise the person and when that person is ready to be prepared for this role, then I will take it from there. This will be someone who is dedicated, who is committed, someone who is in sync and in rapport with spiritual life. Then I will show them the way, just as I was shown the way when I was ready. There will always be dedicated people here to run the place though, I am very confident about that, and that is what is important for now. The administration will go on, but continuing the spiritual tradition is important.

'Of course I don't see this place apart from Munger – what happens here cannot be done in isolation from Munger because they are both the creation of Swami Satyananda, so in that respect I see it as a combined effort. Because for me to have a successor here, and for Swami Niranjan to have a successor there, that creates a separation. So it has to be common. If Swami Niranjan has a successor, it doesn't mean it is only for Munger. And the person who is chosen for Rikhia, has to be very much connected with Munger. I am very much oriented with Munger, I know everything there. Tomorrow if I have to take up the place, I can do it, because I know everything there. It's the same with Swami Niranjan, he knows everything here. This is how we have functioned from the beginning. So it has to be the same in terms of a successor. There may be two successors, one for there and one for here, but they have to have this approach.

'Secondly, I always feel that for this place, a female is needed, rather than a male because of the female energy. The reason I could get this success is because I'm a female; if I was a male I would not get this success. So from that point of view, I still have that in my mind and I still have to know if I'm right in that. I'm not sure about it because with females it's very difficult, females have a nature which is full of attachments. A person who has to succeed here has to have a different kind of nature, no attachments, I could overcome that. And this is the condition which Swamiji placed before me. He said, "To take *sannyas* is okay, everyone takes *sannyas*. Women, they are very insecure and they are very attached, and they have a lot of attachments, and this is what restricts their growth. They may have all the understanding of spiritual life, they may be understanding, compassionate, they may have love, they may be hard-working and dedicated but attachment comes and then they can't see anything more. For Indian women, it's much more, for Westerners, it's much less." So he said, "You have to prove to me that you are independent and that's not a binding factor in your life. You may be financially independent, but emotional independence? We always find a crutch somewhere. You have to prove those things to me, and then only think of *sannyas*."

'So I also set the same guidelines for a successor. I expect the same from a person who has to succeed me. Whether it's male or female I can't say, but definitely this place is more attuned to the female energy. The *Sat Chandi Yagya,* where offerings are made to God in the form of the Divine Mother, was here, the Shakti Peeth is here, plus my contribution. It's also the heart centre. So I feel a female will fit in more, but there are also many males who have a combination of nature, where they are not very aggressive, so it could be anybody. But the only condition is that there has to be a degree of detachment, this is very much needed in spiritual life. Even though there are *sannyasins*, they have strong attachments. They may leave attachments to family, but then they have attachment to the guru, sometimes they even have attachment to the department they are given, they become so egoistic about it, it doesn't work. You have to overcome these things, you have to work on yourself, such a person is needed for spiritual life.

'I uphold a spiritual tradition, not just a secular tradition, where there is an institution and service is being given. The foundation is spiritual and in spiritual life, *vairagya* is very, very important. *Vairagya,* non-attachment, *tyaag,* renunciation, and *samarpan,* surrender. If I see these qualities in anybody, then that is what I look out for.'

~

BP: 'What did you find unique in Swami Satyananda?'
SS: 'What I found unique about him is that he accepted people as they are, he did not try to tell you how you should be. He accepted you as you are and then he made you useful. That was the most unique factor that I found in him. The second unique factor was that he always picked up people who were useless, who were virtually good-for-nothing and he

made them useful. He said that is an achievement... if I take a useful person and give him something to do then what is my contribution? After all, what was I? Just an ordinary girl, who had graduated and just doing an ordinary job. There are a thousand million people like that. Everyone you see here, they were not qualified for the roles that they undertake now. The people you see now leading construction projects or working with the local communities to determine what projects need to take priority, they were not at all qualified for that. But Swami Satyananda, he gave them that dignity, status, an importance, a usefulness, he could so readily identify people's strengths and bring those out. He did not focus on weaknesses and try to correct them, he focused on the positive in people and get the best out of them, and in so doing he gave them immense confidence to achieve things that were beyond their imagining before they came to the ashram. This is such a rare quality that Swamiji had, a quality I didn't find in other people. Swamiji always tried to help the people who were downtrodden, who really had nothing going for them and make them successful. So that was a very important aspect of his personality.

'Another thing I found in him which was unique was that he drew out the best in a person. Everybody could give their life for him without thinking, they would not do it for anybody else. If Swamiji had to tell anybody anything, that person would turn everything upside down to do it, even if at first they thought it was well beyond their capacity. This was something very rare as well.

'Of course, Swami Satyananda was a great intellect with great spiritual accomplishments – he was a *siddha*, he had attained enlightenment, he was enlightened from birth. That is also rare, you don't find people like that every day. But despite that, his extraordinary simplicity, he lived like such a simple person to the last day of his life; the room where he lived, the clothes he used to wear, just two small dhotis and nothing else, not silk nor satin, just ordinary coarse dhotis. In his room he did not even have a fan, just two bare rooms, that was all, no comforts. To be able to live like that when you have the whole world ready to do anything for you, that is a rare quality.

'Another rare quality of his was that he was always correct. Whatever he did, I have not found a person like that. I could never say that anything that Swamiji did or said was not correct. It may not have been palatable for somebody, but it was always correct. He abided by truth and he always did the correct thing. That correctness was not something limited to that moment, it was something which he could see in the future. He could see that in the future this person is going to need that. At that time, you could not realise it. But now, twenty years later, the things that I'm seeing come to fruition, how he planted the seeds of creation, how he made us aware. At that time it just seemed like ordinary things, but how crucial they are to our growth, this I saw in him also, his remarkable foresight. And everything he did, he did very casually, he never made a big show about anything. You may not have even given it importance or registered it properly, but it was something which was very correct for that person. He was such a remarkable visionary.

'No matter what I say, it's not enough. What I've said is just a tip of the surface, there is so much more about him. When you say it, it does not have the gravity. Words are never enough to convey who he was, it's something that you can only really experience. So it's difficult really to say what was so unique about him. Every little thing about him was unique. Even his smile was unique, even the way he walked, the way he stood, the way he looked at you. Every act, everything of his was meaningful. If he just looked at you, it was meaningful and your whole day changed after that. I don't think I will ever find another person like that, it is just impossible.

'And now the only desire I have is that in every life, for every life, for all time, I am just with him. In whichever way and whatever way. That is the only thing that I want now, and nothing else. That I never lose sight of him and that I'm always with him in every life, and keep moving on and evolving. There's no other desire, no other craving, nothing. The only thing is that I have to hold on to this, what I have received by some grace. And in every life I should have this. Even when I'm not alive, when I'm existing somewhere, some way, I must have contact with him. That I don't want to lose. That is the most important thing for me. I have realised that the guru is the most important person – without the guru, nothing can happen.'

BP: 'Is there anything that you think the people should know about?'

SS: 'The importance of the guru should be known, not just in the spiritual self, but in every individual. The guru is like the touchstone that actually polishes the metal. Until the guru comes in your life you cannot attain that. If somebody doesn't have a guru now in his life, it's okay, he's successful, he's earning money, he has his family and everything... but at some point he will feel that something is missing, and then at some point he will look for that. When the guru comes, then his life becomes complete, until then, there is always some incompleteness. Whether you are materially or spiritually inclined, or a combination of both, the importance of the guru is utmost. This is the most important factor in my life, in the life of Swami Niranjan and in the life of Swami Satyananda.

'I never asked Swami Satyananda for any advice. I never asked him anything, but I got all my answers, and that is how a disciple needs to be. A disciple can't be sitting and asking the guru all the questions and chewing his head. The process is of transmission, you have to build that connection with the guru, and when you have that connection with your guru, then there's no problem. Then the guru shows you through different ways, certain things happen, certain books you read, certain things that somebody says, something clicks and you know that it's the guru talking through that person. So it's a process of transmission, sometimes nobody is talking and then a thought comes to you; an idea comes, the guru plants that idea in you and then you begin to think in that way. The guru can only do that if you are open to the process of transmission, and for that the guru is always checking the disciple, how aware is he. Many times he may knock on you but you're not even aware, you're thinking of something else, then he leaves you. According to that, the guru teaches the disciple.

'So when you say that there are people who take *diksha*, initiation, and go away, their awareness is different. Swami Niranjan's awareness was different, my awareness was different, and according to that the guru gives the training and teaching and creates the link. So it's the guru actually who decides, not the disciple. He checks the disciple's evolution, the disciple's awareness, what are the things where he gets caught, how strong maya is on him, what are his compulsions. Then he gives the teaching. But at the same time, he's always giving the teaching in such a way, that even the person who's not aware gradually comes to a process of becoming aware, so that the person also grows. With the guru, it's always a matter of the evolution of the disciple. Even an unevolved disciple who is not at all aware, who has just taken the *diksha* and has forgotten about it, even he gains from it. Because he has in some way made a link and then the guru takes that link forward.

'But, of course, when a disciple does not respond at all, then such a disciple will be discarded. But a guru is very patient, and he gives a lot of rope to the disciple, he puts a lot of time and effort into that. But even when he rejects such a disciple, he guides that person in a way that his destiny unfolds in front of him, some avenue will still open up for him. So contact with the guru is always beneficial. Some disciples may not evolve spiritually because there is an obstruction in their life to achieve what they want, but that also clears.

'With Swami Niranjan and me he allowed us that proximity. With Swami Niranjan it was from childhood, he was born literally in his lap and although he lived apart from him for a long period, that was also a part of his grace and his plan for him. He wanted him to become independent, because to live under Swami Satyananda from a young age he may have developed a feeling of awe and his growth may have been stifled. He allowed Swami Niranjan to live in foreign countries, with foreign cultures and learn about other people. Then he called him back. It's not like he used to write letters to him or call him, but when that contact is there, the transmission process continued, where he was guiding him, sending him ideas and thoughts which were beneficial for his growth. Swami Niranjan used to say that he used to talk about subjects which he didn't even know, so where did all that come from? Definitely, the guru was opening all the locks of the brain. Then when he came back, Swami Satyananda left Munger, so actually Swami Niranjan hardly really lived with Swamiji, yet, his influence was always with him, guiding him continuously on his way.

'My nature was quite different from Swami Niranjan's and, of course, I came to Swami Satyananda at a much later age. I needed that close proximity with Swamiji to develop into the role that I have now and I was crucial in supporting Swamiji in his sadhana, I was there to ensure the ashram could run on a daily basis without concerning him about this. From childhood Swamiji would have worked on Swami Niranjan and when he reached the age of ten he was ready to go out in the world. Whereas I came at a time where I had to catch up, I was lagging so much behind. And even today I would say I'm lagging behind – I don't think I've reached anywhere, I need to pick up on so many things. It's a constant process. Certainly I do not think that I've become so accomplished where I don't need to learn anything. I still feel I need to learn, I always need to be aware of that process and keep myself open to that. I still feel that. But Swamiji gave me that proximity, he gave me that chance and he encouraged me to be myself, and not be someone I need to be because I'm in his presence. He encouraged me to be outspoken, to express my mind. Most of the disciples, in front of Swami Satyananda, they would just be silent, but I was always talking. He always used to encourage me, and if ever I was silent he always used to ask me, "So Satsangi, what do you think about that?" and I used to start off, because I was just being myself. Perhaps there was some use in that, because he knew that some time I had to be on my own and in the role that I had to play I would have to assert myself. Bihar is certainly not the easiest place, especially for a lady. He wanted me to be more assertive and strong, so he encouraged that in me.

'And then there were times when there was Swami Niranjan, Swamiji and me, and he used to talk about everything under the sun. It wasn't just spiritual things, he talked about the mind and nature, geography and history, politics, science, art, astronomy and just normal things like cooking as well. And we used to just listen to him, it used to be so beautiful. And in that way he built a bond between us, because I didn't know Swami Niranjan – he used to be living abroad. When I came to the ashram, he was in America, he came later. So I didn't know him at all, he was virtually a stranger to me. But the common bond was Swamiji and he created that bond between us, and this is so important for us today. We hardly meet, but whenever we meet, it's like we were never apart. I give that credit to Swamiji, because otherwise to have such a strong bond with somebody is not possible with just your own effort. It's like in a friendship, but any little thing can create a misunderstanding, and then that friendship breaks. You work so hard for friendship, you work so hard for a relationship, but then one small thing and it breaks. But our understanding of each other is beyond that, nothing can break that feeling which I have for Swami Niranjan because for me he represents my guru. I cannot go against that, I cannot ever think anything against that. For me it is like Swamiji is Swami Niranjan. They are not apart from each other for me. For me they are the same, although they may be in two different bodies. Of course, he's not my guru, he's my *guru bhai*, so I don't seek any advice from him, nor does he guide me. But there's a different feeling, I don't know how to explain it. It's not the kind of relationship we know about, it's something which Swamiji ignited between us.

'Even if we are miles apart, if there is something happening, I can know it. Like when he went to Kailash, at that time they had some difficulty – the whole night and the whole morning I was very restless. Usually he was calling me and telling me everything, but that day he didn't call and finally, I couldn't contain myself and I just sent a message and asked if everything was okay. That day they had some incident where a horse had trampled somebody who was on that journey. That man literally came out from the hands of death. That whole morning Swamiji was looking to me as very serious, Shiva was looking very serious, so I was sure that something was wrong. The next day Swami Niranjan called and narrated the whole incident, because he had not even replied to my message. So I could feel everything. Then after that when he had the *darshan* there, I also had the *darshan* of Shiva here.

'So I can't explain this. It's not something which is logical. This was more or less the feeling which I had with Swamiji where I could intuitively know things. The only thing I couldn't know, was his exit. This he blocked in my mind. I did know it, but he used to keep blocking it. I remember two days before he took *samadhi* I even asked him, "Swamiji, are you planning to go somewhere?" And he just looked at me… there was a moment when it was him and me, I was thinking he's going to Rishikesh. And I asked him, "Swamiji, are you planning to go somewhere? Are you planning to leave Rikhia?" and the look which he gave me… I just froze. Usually I would never ask him, I would never say something like that. And then somebody came and he didn't answer me. And after that the thought just disappeared from my mind. I didn't have that thought again. So he realised that something was coming to me, and he blocked it because he didn't want us to know. I wouldn't have been able to manage. The way in which he did it, that was the best way. To know a day before that he was going to leave his body, I wouldn't have survived that day. So he just knew our nature and the way that we would react, and so he did it that way. He allowed us to know in the way that he allowed us to know. And that also, like I said, he always did everything very correctly. There's always the thought that, "Swamiji why didn't you tell me?", but I knew that would not have been the right way. This was the right way, and he did it that way.

'He told me only that night when he called me. He didn't tell me what he was planning, but I was picking something up. In some moments I used to pick up his thoughts and then he used to block it. Now when I look back on it, there was high emotion at that time – I was feeling very, very emotional at that time. I didn't know why I was feeling that way. Now when I look back, well I realise now of course why it was. But at that time I didn't know. Only when he called me to his room, only then I knew. That day he spent in the most natural way, he was not in any panic or any hurry or turmoil like how we would be. If we knew that we had to leave, we would not have the clarity of mind to do anything. He just lived it like a normal day, we could not read anything into the situation.

'And so, I have been on an incredible and fascinating journey, and am still on it. It's far from ended.'

Postscript

'My Name is Sita'

Chaitra Navaratri, *the festival of nine nights that marks the beginning of summer, is observed each year at the Rikhia ashram. For nine nights and ten days, several hundreds of visitors congregate there and participate in this elaborate occasion that celebrates Devi, the Divine Mother.*

On the final night of this occasion in 2014, I asked Sita, Nitu, Sonu and Puja, all teenage college students now, to tell me what Swami Satsangi and the ashram meant to them. Though each of these young women can be seen at the forefront of many of the events in the ashram, addressing thousands in English and Hindi with confidence and authority, they are beautifully innocent, shy girls at heart. Speaking softly, they told me that the ashram was like their home and they felt blessed to have had the opportunity to have grown up within this environment. Their mothers who were also there told me, with tears in their eyes, how extremely grateful they were for all that they had experienced because of Swami Satsangi and the ashram.

We said our goodbyes and I resolved to include their message in Swami Satsangi's story. To my surprise, as I was preparing to leave the ashram around six am the following morning, I found Sita waiting for me, along with Sinu, a young woman who now works in a bank.

When Sita had returned home after our conversation the previous evening, she had prepared two pages in beautifully handwritten Hindi what the ashram meant to her. While waiting for me, she and Sinu were busily translating the piece into English. Her words clearly convey what she, and all the people of Rikhia have gained from the presence of Swami Satsangi in their lives...

My name is Sita. I was born during the Rajsuya Yajna in 1996 and Sri Swamiji gave me my name. I have been coming to the ashram all my life. Even since I started speaking I have been learning how to chant and, for many years, I have been chanting the *Shantipath* in all programmes. Sri Swamiji sat me next to him for every one of the *satsang* and programmes. When Sri Swamiji used to go for his walks, I always used to bow down to him. It was as if he would call me himself to bless me for I always knew in which direction he would go for his walk.

Today, we are able to chant only because Swami Satsangi taught us everything. She taught us each and every chant with great effort and efficiency and, as a result, our chanting and *kirtans* have been appreciated by Sri Swamiji, Swami Niranjanji and many other people. Swami Satsangi loves us very much and takes care of us. We get beautiful dresses in all programmes and after wearing them we look very beautiful. It feels as if we are the most fashionable children in the world.

In the ashram, we have eaten all kinds of Western food and by being in ashram we have met people from all over the world and have come to know about their cultures. I feel like Sri Swamiji brought the entire world to Rikhia for us – we can wish for a bright future by being in the ashram.

The atmosphere of the ashram influences me so much that I don't want to go to my house but prefer to stay in the ashram instead. I feel like this is my first home to which I started coming soon as I came into this world.

Sometimes I think of children who do not have a great yogi like Sri Swamiji in their lives or who have not known a follower like Swami Niranjanji whose life is a living example of discipleship, or a kind, caring and generous disciple like Swami Satsangiji. Swami Satsangi takes great care of us and it is because of her that I am able to speak before you in English.

Swami Satsangi is our role model and mentor, who takes care of us like our mother. She has instilled good values in us. We love her very, very, very much and, from the bottom of our hearts, we wish to walk the path she has shown us and become what she wants us to be. I really consider myself blessed to have received the guidance, love, compassion and blessings of Sri Swamiji at every step and wish the same from Swami Satsangi and Swami Niranjanji. I can only try to express in words the beautiful and priceless moments that we have experienced... but such moments cannot be bound in language and can hardly be expressed in words.

Sita

Rikhia
8 April 2014

Acknowledgements

I would like to record my heartfelt thanks to everyone at the Rikhia Ashram for all the support given to me that enabled the writing of this book, and my utmost appreciation also to Dr Baxi and Dr Hilton who took the time to review a draft and provide their valued written contributions.

I am humbled that the young *kanya*, Sita, on her own initiative, took the time to write a beautiful tribute to how her life has been impacted by the unforeseen arrival of Swami Satyananda and Swami Satsangi at Rikhia.

Most of all though, no words could adequately convey my gratitude to Swami Satsangi, and I would like to thank her for making her time available to me to discuss the development of this book and for the impact this has had on my personal growth. Her guidance was instrumental in how this book took shape.

I feel incredibly honoured that, despite all the demands

made on them on a daily basis, Swami Niranjan and Swami Satsangi provided their personal inputs to what is now before us.

Om Tat Sat

References

Swami Dayananda Saraswati, 2012, *Bhagavad Gita Home Study Course,* Arsha Vidya Research and Publication Trust, Mylapore, Chennai, India.

Swami Niranjananda Saraswati, 1999, *Dharana Darshan,* Yoga Publications Trust, Munger, Bihar, India.

Swami Niranjananda Saraswati, 2008, *Sannyasa Darshan,* Yoga Publications Trust, Munger, Bihar, India.

Swami Niranjananda Saraswati, 2010, *Mantra and Yantra,* Yoga Publications Trust, Munger, Bihar, India.

Swami Niranjananda Saraswati, 2012, *The Yoga of Sage Vasishtha,* Yoga Publications Trust, Munger, Bihar, India.

Swami Niranjananda Saraswati, 2013, *Tantra Darshan,* Yoga Publications Trust, Munger, Bihar, India.

Swami Satyananda Saraswati, 2009, *Bhakti Yoga Sagar, Volume One,* Yoga Publications Trust, Munger, Bihar, India.

Swami Satyananda Saraswati, 2001, *Bhakti Yoga Sagar, Volume Two,* Yoga Publications Trust, Munger, Bihar, India.

Swami Satyananda Saraswati, 2007, *Bhakti Yoga Sagar, Volume Three,* Yoga Publications Trust, Munger, Bihar, India.

Swami Satyananda Saraswati, 2007, *Bhakti Yoga Sagar, Volume Four,* Yoga Publications Trust, Munger, Bihar, India.

Swami Satyananda Saraswati, 2006, *Bhakti Yoga Sagar, Volume Five,* Yoga Publications Trust, Munger, Bihar, India.

Swami Satyananda Saraswati, 2001, *Bhakti Yoga Sagar, Volume Six,* Yoga Publications Trust, Munger, Bihar, India.

Swami Satyananda Saraswati, 2001, *Bhakti Yoga Sagar, Volume Seven,* Yoga Publications Trust, Munger, Bihar, India.

Swami Satyananda Saraswati, 2009, *Rikhiapeeth Satsangs,* Yoga Publications Trust, Munger, Bihar, India.

Swami Satyananda Saraswati, 2009, *Rikhiapeeth Satsangs 2,* Yoga Publications Trust, Munger, Bihar, India.

Swami Satyasangananda Saraswati, 1983, *Light on the Guru and Disciple Relationship,* Yoga Publications Trust, Munger, Bihar, India.

Swami Satyasangananda Saraswati, 2003, *Sri Vijnana Bhairava Tantra The Ascent,* Yoga Publications Trust, Munger, Bihar, India.

Swami Satyasangananda Saraswati, 2009, *Sri Saundarya Lahari, The Descent,* Yoga Publications Trust, Munger, Bihar, India.

Rikhiapeeth, 2012, *Ram Naam Aradhana,* Rikhiapeeth, P.O. Rikhia, Dist. Deoghar, Jharkand, India.

Rikhiapeeth, 2012, *Devi Sahasranam,* Rikhiapeeth, P.O. Rikhia, Dist. Deoghar, Jharkand, India.

Rikhiapeeth, 2012, *ARADHANA Yoga of the heart, Issue 3,* Swami Gyantara Saraswati.

Rikhiapeeth, 2012, *ARADHANA Yoga of the heart, Issue 5,* Swami Gyantara Saraswati.

Rikhiapeeth, 2013, *ARADHANA Yoga of the heart, Issue 4,* Swami Gyantara Saraswati

Teachings from Swami Sivananda Saraswati and Swami Satyananda Saraswati, 2007, *Devi Honouring Shakti,* Yoga Publications Trust, Munger, Bihar, India.

Swami Kriyananda, 2011, *Paramhansa Yogananda, A Biography,* Crystal Clarity Publishers, Nevada City, USA.

C. J. Jung (Edited by J.J. Clarke), 1995, *Jung on the East,* Routledge, London, UK.

K. Suresh Chandar, 2010, *Jagadguru Sri Adi Shankara,* Vidya Bharati Press.

Sivarupa, 2012, *Yogis of India, Timeless Stories of Their Lives and Wisdom,* Wisdom Tree, New Delhi, India.

Swati Chopra, 2011, *Women Awakened, Stories of Contemporary Spirituality in India,* HarperCollins, Noida, India.

Satyananda Magazine Publications:

Swami Yogamaya Saraswati, 2012, *Satya ka Avahan, Issue 5,* Sannyasa Peeth, Ganga Darshan, Munger, Bihar, India.

Swami Yogamaya Saraswati, 2013, *Satya ka Avahan, Issue 4,* Sannyasa Peeth, Ganga Darshan, Munger, Bihar, India.

Swami Yogatirthananda Saraswati, 2012, *YOGA, Issue 4,* Bihar School of Yoga, Munger, Bihar, India.

Swami Yogatirthananda Saraswati, 2012, *YOGA, Issue 10,* Bihar School of Yoga, Munger, Bihar, India.